WITH MANY MIRACLES

WITH MANY MIRACLES

A Memoir
of
Holocaust Survival
in
Belgium

ISRAEL CAPPELL

KAPELUSZNIK & CO.

With Many Miracles
A Memoir of Holocaust Survival in Belgium

By Israel Cappell

© Copyright 2023 Ken Cappell

ISBN: 979-8-218-34600-3

Cover design by Jason Anscomb.

Book design and layout by Elliott Beard.

Published by
Kapelusznik & Co.

In memory of our parents Israel Cappell (1922–2021)
and Evelyn Cappell (1924–2017)

and our sister Netty Gross-Horowitz (1954–2021)

Michele Bankhalter and Ken Cappell

CONTENTS

EDITORS' NOTE

THIS MANUSCRIPT HAS PASSED through many hands, and its publication owes a debt to many parties.

Israel Cappell (1922-2021) composed his memoirs by hand, in a series of spiral notebooks in the years before his death. Israel's daughter, Netty C. Gross-Horowitz (née Cappell, 1954–2021), a talented writer and journalist, was driven to bring the memoir to publication. In roughly the mid-2000s, she began a process of transcribing, annotating, editing, and modestly expanding the work. She also published a compelling feature on her father in *The Jerusalem Post International Edition* ("Last Address Unknown," January 21, 1995). (See appendix.) In 2013, Netty emailed her close friend Janine Zacharia that: "my father, 91, is very excited [at the prospect that his memoir may be published] but worried that he might not live to see the result!!!"

After Netty's tragic death in 2021, Netty's brother Ken Cappell spoke with Janine, a mentee and colleague of Netty's (at the Jerusalem Report) of his desire to have his father's wartime memoir published. Janine, in an effort to honor Netty and Israel, whom she also knew personally, wanted to complete Netty's unfinished task and graciously agreed to reanimate and support this effort.

Janine in turn invited Sarah Abrevaya Stein, who has written and taught extensively about Holocaust history, to join the endeavor. Janine and Sarah also have long roots together, having met in Jerusalem as students who could not yet imagine the journalistic and scholarly careers they would soon launch.

Sarah, in turn, involved a third generation of aspiring scholars in the effort to bring Israel's words to print. UCLA undergraduates Michaela Esposito, Maia Gelerter, Gillian Smith, as well as UCLA Visiting Graduate Researcher Ann (Xiaoxu) Pei, brought enormous energy, creativity, and sensitivity to the project—pursuing every imaginable historical thread and debating the ethics of each editorial choice. Thanks to the UCLA Alan D. Leve Center for Jewish Studies and the Sady and Ludwig Kahn Chair for supporting these students' efforts.

We have tried to acknowledge the imprint of all these parties on the manuscript. Israel Cappell's words have been given center stage, and the editors have used an intentionally light hand such that his voice speaks loudest. We have standardized proper nouns, punctuation, and dates and times; entered clarifying footnotes when necessary; and corrected misspellings from foreign languages. We have also moved some digressionary material into footnotes and introduced an editors' note to prepare the reader for a flashback. In all cases, our goal was to doctor Israel's voice as little as possible, while making the memoir readable and accessible.

Within the text, content in square brackets has been introduced by the editors for clarity (e.g., "*arichat yamim* [Hebrew, literally length of days, aka a long life]'). Throughout, "I.C." refers to content authored by Israel Cappell, and "N.G." refers to content authored by Netty Gross-Horowitz. Editors' notes are marked as such. Netty Gross-Horowitz's research bibliography has been updated and expanded to produce a recommended bibliography at the book's end.

To complement Israel's memoir, we have included a Cast of Characters list (produced by Michaela Esposito, Maia Gelerter, Ann (Xiaoxu) Pei, and Gillian Smith), and a map of his and his family's movements (produced by Bill Nelson). Additionally, Sarah has provided a framing introduction, Ken, an homage to his father and an explanation of the cover and title, Ken's sister, Michele, an homage to their mother, and Janine, an homage to Netty.

We believe Israel would appreciate that his memoir has at last found print, that it has inspired an intergenerational effort, and that it honors the life of his extraordinary daughter as well as his own.

Sarah Abrevaya Stein
Janine Zacharia

ACKNOWLEDGEMENTS

MY FATHER, ISRAEL CAPPELL, began writing this memoir in 2012 when he was eighty years old. He wanted to leave a legacy for his descendants but was also interested in publishing it for a wider audience. For a variety of reasons, it never was published until now, a little over two years since his passing. He wrote it by hand and subsequently my sister Netty Gross-Horowitz retyped it on a computer, shaped and edited it. Netty was a noted journalist and writer living in Israel and it's unlikely that this book would exist without her herculean effort to get this memoir in a format suitable for publication. I and my family are forever indebted to her, and we are saddened that she did not live to see this day.

When Netty passed away in November 2021, I received a call from her close friend and former colleague, Janine Zacharia. As noted in the Editors' Note, after mentioning my desire to publish my father's book, Janine explained how much she loved my sister and my parents and wanted to complete Netty's unfinished edit. She brought her skills, experience, professionalism, creativity, ideas, and contacts to the project. She was all-in and her leadership of the project was critical to its completion. It was a pleasure working with her and she has my eternal thanks for making my father's dream come true.

At Janine's suggestion, we engaged Sarah Abrevaya Stein, Professor of History and the Viterbi Family Chair in Mediterranean Jewish Studies, and the Sady and Ludwig Kahn Director of the Alan D. Leve Center for Jewish Studies at UCLA. Sarah, an author of many books on the Holocaust brought her expertise and prodigious knowledge to offer ideas how to improve my father's story and put it into the context of the Holocaust experience in Belgium. Sarah not only brought her scholarship to bear, but also offered pragmatic wisdom which helped immensely. She also engaged her students Michaela Esposito, Maia Gelerter, Ann (Xiaoxu) Pei, and Gillian Smith, to fact check the events in the book, clarify foreign phrases and terms, create timelines, and bring the book to life. I am so grateful for Sarah and her students. Their contributions turned a rough draft into a sparkling gem.

I would also like to thank Jason Anscomb who designed the beautiful cover and Elliott Beard who did a marvelous job with the book design and layout and exhibited great patience with any last-minute changes. Finally, special thanks to my sister Michele Bankhalter who provided her thoughts and suggestions throughout the process and to my wife Marcie and my children and extended family members for their overall support.

Ken Cappell
June 2023

Israel Cappell's Wartime History in Context

ISRAEL CAPPELL WAS BORN in Łódź (Lodz) in May of 1922. His native city, located in the heart of Poland, was a bustling industrial center and home to the second largest Jewish community in prewar Poland. On the eve of World War Two, this community numbered over 200,000 and accounted for a third of the city's overall population. Łódź was a city of textile mills and poets, yeshivas and bookstores, crowded streets lined with trams and the residual horse–drawn carriage. The city's Jewish culture was rich and dense, with myriad theaters, libraries, political organizations, Hasidic *shtiebels* [prayer houses], and more. Israel's childhood address, 22 Piotrkowska, was equidistant from the Reicher synagogue, the impressive mansion of Izrael Poznański Palace (or Izraela Poznańskiego, a nineteenth century Jewish cotton mogul), and the Louvre Restaurant, which was fronted by an overflowing newspaper stand. Around him was all of Łódź's riches.

His maternal grandfather, Israel Taub, the first Modzhitser rebbe, was revered both as a rebbe and as a composer of Hasidic *nigunim* [musical compositions], a musical talent that would pass to his son and grandson in time. Israel's paternal grandfather, who carried the

The Kapelusznik family's pre-war neighborhood: 86 Piotrkowska
Street, Łódź, Poland, 1930, courtesy Wiki Images.

family's original name, Chaim Wolf Kapelusznik, was an industrialist
remembered for his philanthropic spirit. The family bore the imprint
of Łódź's dual Jewish traditions—religious and cultural effervescence,
and industrial entrepreneurism.

While the mass emigration of Eastern European Jewry had been
forcibly slowed by 1930, still there was much intra-continental movement. The Kapelusznik/Cappell family joined the tide in 1930 with a
move westward, to the Belgian capital of Brussels, perhaps lured by the
city's thriving textile industry. Flemish- and French-speaking; secular,
Catholic, Protestant, and minority Jewish; Brussels was rapidly chang-
ing at this pre-war moment, particularly from the vantage of its Jewish
community.

Brussels was home to a diverse Jewish population of some 50,000
when the family arrived. The city contained more than half of Belgium's Jews. Historically, Brussels's Jewish community had been made
up of waves of Sephardic and Ashkenazi migrants. Its earliest immigrants came from the Netherlands and Germany, while its more recent,

twentieth century immigrants—more working class and religiously observant than those that preceded them—arrived from Russia and Poland. With the rise of the Nazi party, a new wave of Jews arrived from Germany. This inflow of migrants increased the size of Belgium's Jewish community from just 10,000 prior to the First World War to 50,000 in 1930 and 70–75,000 by the spring of 1940. An astonishingly small 5% of Jews living in Belgium at the outset of the war held Belgian nationality: the Cappell/Kapeluszniks, for their part, retained their Polish nationality, never acquiring Belgian nationality.

Brussels was a far smaller city than Israel's native Łódź, and its Jewish community far less numerous, but Jewish life in Brussels was active and diverse. There was a rich Jewish literary world (especially in Yiddish), a Jewish theater, and various Jewish political movements, including Bnei Akiva (The Sons of Akiva), a religious Zionist youth movement to which Israel belonged. In contrast to nearby Antwerp, Brussels did not have any Jewish schools, but the city could claim many synagogues. Alas, this inflow of immigrants fueled xenophobic and anti-Semitic political parties in Belgium, which gained popularity in the 1930s.

The Third Reich conquered neutral Belgium in May of 1940, as part of its invasion of Western Europe. In a few short weeks, the Belgian government sought safe haven in London and King Leopold III ordered the surrender of the Belgian army, while he himself remained under house arrest in Belgium. In Belgium, the Nazi regime established a German military administration (the *Militärverwaltung*) headed by a German general, Alexander von Falkenhausen and staffed by senior German administrators, including the powerful Eggert Reeder. This imposed military infrastructure existed alongside the Belgian civil service, which supported the German occupiers inconsistently, and remained in place until nearly the end of the war.

As the Allies and Axis powers were still fighting for control over Belgium (sometime between May 10 and 28, 1940), many Jews including the Cappell/Kapelusznik family—Israel, his parents Jacob Emanuel and Sarah Esther Kapelusznik, his brother Charles, and two of his sisters Fanny (Feigele) and Regine (Rifka), and their husbands, and

Section of Israel Cappell's post-war Belgian work permit, listing him as a Polish national, 1947, courtesy Ken Cappell

Section of Jacob Kapelusznik's post-war Polish passport, 1947, courtesy Ken Cappell

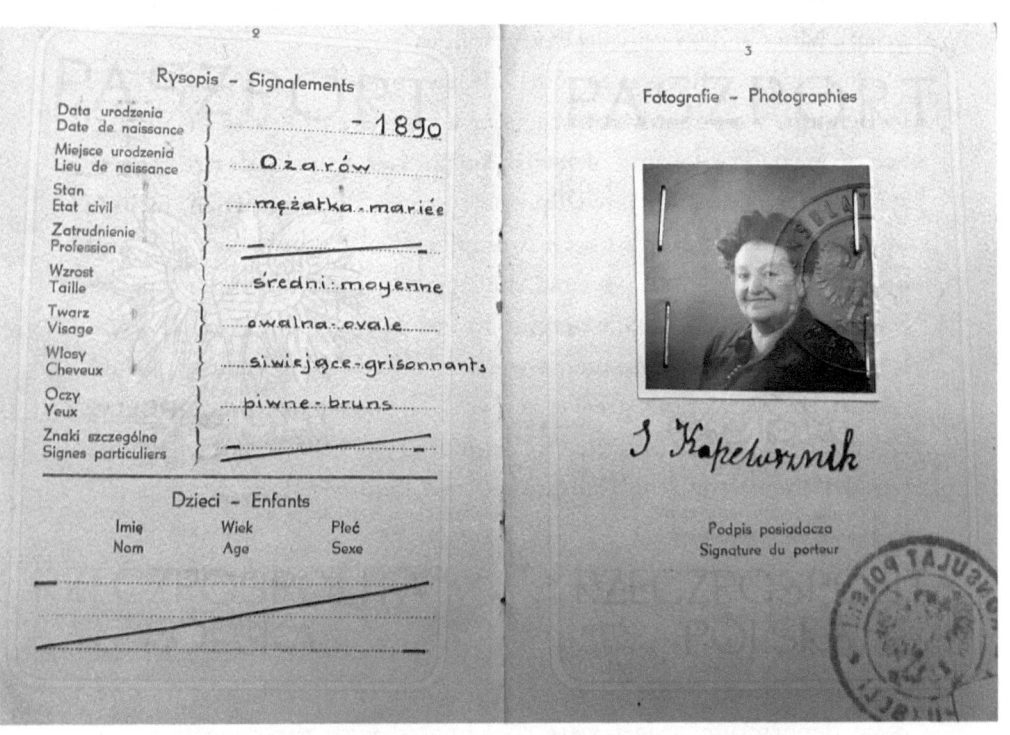

Section of Sarah Esther ("Sura Estera") Kapelusznik's
post-war Polish passport, 1947, courtesy Ken Cappell

one infant—tried to flee westward, to France. After a cinematic and failed venture, they returned home and entered a year of suspended stasis and diminishing opportunity.

Immediately after German forces occupied Belgium, they initiated the deportation of some German Jewish émigrés living in Belgium, along with non-Jewish political refugees, and sent these perceived "undesirables" to internment camps in southern France (Gurs and St. Cyprien). More violent policies would follow.

In a sign of what was to come, all Jews over the age of 15 who lived in Belgium were required to register with the authorities in December of 1940. The looting of Jewish businesses and the destruction of synagogues and other Jewish property soon followed. Then, in June of 1941, the Third Reich began to implement its anti-Jewish laws and ordinances in Belgium. At first, the legislation was cutting but petty: Jews were forbidden from keeping radios and pigeons. A curfew was imposed, and Jews' movements were curtailed. With each successive month, the restrictions grew in severity. The occupying powers confiscated Jewish-owned property in Belgium, restricted Jews' civil rights, banned them from the professions, and required them to wear the yellow Star of David.

In the late summer of 1942, the German authorities began a policy of raids and mass arrests—at first in Antwerp (in August, 1942) and then in Brussels (in September, 1942). On the heels of these actions, the deportations began. They would continue through July 31, 1944. Nazi deportation orders were coordinated with the deportation of Jews from the Netherlands and France and emanated from Adolf Eichmann's Reich Security Main Office (*Reichssicherheitshauptamt,* or RSHA). These orders were handled by the small, Nazi-appointed Bureau of Jewish Affairs and were carried out by German *Feldgendarmerie* (military police). At their hands, approximately 25,500 Jewish women, men, and children, (along with 350 Roma and Sinti) would be taken from their homes, and sent primarily to the internment camp at Mechelen. Located at the site of a former army barracks in Mechelen, halfway between Antwerp and Brussels and on a train line, the camp of Mechelen was repurposed in March of 1942 as Belgium's only Nazi transit camp. SS-Sammellager Mechelen was also known as the Kazerne Dossin.

In many respects it was typical of Nazi transit camps elsewhere in Europe. Rates of survival for those who spent time in Mechelen prior to their deportation were particularly low. Its captives were mostly Jews and most of those interned were sent from Mechelen to Auschwitz-Birkenau. Twenty-eight transports left Mechelen for Auschwitz, and of the more than 25,000 deported, only 1,240 survived the war. An additional 500 or so prisoners of Mechelen managed to escape the camp or the transports.

Over 25,000 Jewish individuals living in Belgium during this peril-

Israel and Evelyn Cappell, circa 1947 courtesy Ken Cappell

ous period managed to hide and evade the deportation orders—sometimes in old-age homes or children's homes. Often those in hiding had the help of non-Jewish Belgians, and occasionally the assistance of members of the civil service. In all, approximately forty to fifty percent of Jews living in Belgium when the war broke out were murdered by the Nazis. Miraculously, Israel Cappell his future wife, Evelyn Isboutsky, and all their siblings and parents, 15 people in total, survived the Holocaust.

Help from non-Jews was among the many miracles that protected Israel and his family. A non-Jew helped transport the family across the French border; non-Jewish doctors treated Israel's scarlet fever in defiance of Nazi law; and non-Jews assisted with the family's concealment in Brussels. That said, it was chance and choice that ultimately determined the fate of the Cappell/Kapelusznik family.

Perhaps the most important choice, rare in Holocaust history, was this: sometime in 1942, Charles took the risky step of registering the family as Zionists with the Brussels Palestine Office, whose leadership he knew from his time in Bnei Akiva. Little could he have known that this act would play a key role in the family's story.

As arrests and deportations of Jews in Belgium mounted, the Cappell/Kapeluszniks and many other Jews went into hiding. Israel describes in detail the experience of hiding from the Nazis—the fear, the precautionary measures, the near misses, the risks, the challenge of bathing or finding kosher (and ample) food, the desperate thirst for news. He also references elusive moments of comfort: the sun on his face; the so-called "situation room" he sets up in an attic, in which he tracks the war's unfolding; and the pleasure of company, particularly that of Pierre Carnewal, a Belgian Catholic member of the resistance whose periodic visits Israel calls "breaths of fresh air."

Alas, moments of respite were the exception not the norm, and the family's fate would soon take a turn for the worse. Shortly after Passover in 1944, the SS raided the family's hiding place on Rue de Châtelain. The dramatic scene that followed represents one of the most suspenseful portions of Israel's memoir. Most of the family was captured, tortured, imprisoned, and sent to the Nazi collection and deportation camp at Kazerne Dossin.

Israel describes the brutality of the mostly Belgian guards at Mechelen—especially one, Von Kohl, whom he nicknames "Ferde Kop" [Yiddish: Horse Head]. Israel's description of life in Mechelen, with its intricate hierarchies and daily humiliations, is both rich and painful. It stands as one of the rare English-language accounts of imprisonment in the Mechelen camp and, for this, is particularly valuable to students of history. How Israel and his family manage to survive is detailed in the most dramatic parts of the memoir.

In his testimony with the Shoah Foundation (though not in his memoir), Israel describes that, upon liberation, the surviving Jewish prisoners organized a spontaneous prayer service to say the *Hallel*, a joyous prayer normally recited on Jewish holidays. And then they set out on foot. After a few hours of walking, British tanks rolled toward them. "To see the British was an unbelievable dream," Israel told his interviewer for the Shoah Foundation. ". . . That was liberation. That was the end of the torture of the last few years of . . . of living an impossible life. And really a series of miracles that saved my life and saved me from going to Auschwitz . . . "

Israel Cappell delivered these words in 1995, his wife Eva at his side, his daughter Michele, and his son Ken, his wife Marcie, and their child Sam in the room. As the interview was drawing to a close, Israel was asked whether he had told his story to his family before. "Well, when they were . . . when my children were little, I . . . I did speak about it. And then when they grew up, they . . . they were not very happy. The reaction was not very happy that I spoke that much about the Holocaust, most of the time because somehow the subject always came up. But now, they all seem to be very interested. . . . And they want to participate in exploring the Holocaust, whatever happened."

It is only due to this steadfast, intergenerational commitment to the past that Israel's memoir comes to light today.

Sarah Abrevaya Stein, UCLA

WORKS CONSULTED BY EDITORS

Unpublished sources

The memoir of Fanny (Feigele) Finkelstein (née Kapelusznik)

The memoir of Suzanne Freeling (née Dyner)

The Kazerne Dossin, Memorial, museum and research centre on
Holocaust and Human rights

USC Shoah Foundation Institute testimony of Israel Cappell, VHA
Interview Code 1502

USC Shoah Foundation Institute testimony of Evelyn Cappell (née
Eva Isboutsky) VHA Interview Code 1501

Published sources

Transport XX to Auschwitz, directors Karen Lynne Bloom, Richard
Bloom (2012).

Sylvain Brachfelt, *Ils ont survécu : Le Sauvetage des Juifs en Belgique
occupée* (Editions Racine, 1997).

Martin Conway, *Collaboration in Belgium: Léon Degrelle and the Rexist
Movement, 1940-1944* (Yale University Press, 1993).

Martin Conway, *The Sorrows of Belgium: Liberation and Political
Reconstruction, 1944-1947* (Oxford University Press, 2012).

Dan Michman, editor, *Belgium and the Holocaust: Jews, Belgians, Germans* (Yad Vashem, 1998).

Dan Michman, editor, *The Encyclopedia of the Righteous Among the Nations (Rescuers of Jews During the Holocaust): Belgium* (Yad Vashem, 2005).

Ann Roekens, *La Belgique et la persécution des Juifs* (Renaissance du Livre, 2010).

Laurence Schram, *Dossin, L'antichambre d'Auschwitz* (Racine, 2016).

Jean-Philippe Schreiber, *Les curateurs du ghetto: L'Association des Juifs en Belgique sous l'occupation nazie* (Editions Labor, 2005).

Maxime Steinberg, *La Persécution des Juifs en Belgique (1940-1945)* (Editions Complexe, 2004).

Jean-Michel Veranneman, *Belgium in the Second World War* (Pen and Sword Military, 2021).

Suzanne Vromen, *Hidden Children of the Holocaust: Belgian Nuns and Their Daring Rescue of Young Jews from the Nazis* (Oxford University Press, 2008).

CHARACTER LIST

Kapelusznik Family

CHARLES (YECHEZKEL) KAPELUSZNIK — Israel's brother.

EVA (EVELYN/ABIGAIL/AVIGAIL) KAPELUSZNIK (*née* ISBOUTSKY) — Israel's wife, whom he met after the war.

FANNY (FEIGELE) FINKELSTEIN (*née* KAPELUSZNIK) — Israel's older sister, married to Josef Finkelstein.

HELEN (CHAYA) DYNER (*née* KAPELUSZNIK) — Israel's oldest sister, married to Jacques Dyner.

JACOB EMANUEL KAPELUSZNIK — Israel's father.

JACQUES (ISRAEL BARUCH) DYNER — Israel's brother-in-law, married to Helen Dyner.

JOSEF FINKELSTEIN — Israel's brother-in-law, married to Fanny Finkelstein.

MAURICE (MOSHE) DYNER — Israel's brother-in-law, married to Regine Dyner.

POLA KAPELUSZNIK (*née* KLEIN) — Israel's sister-in-law, married to Charles after the war.

REGINE (RIFKA) DYNER (*née* KAPELUSZNIK) — Israel's second oldest sister, married to Maurice Dyner.

SARAH ESTHER KAPELUSZNIK — Israel's mother.

SPRINCA (ISA) KAPELUSZNIK (*née* **GLIKSMAN**) — Israel's sister-in-law, Charles' first wife

SUZANNE FREELING (*née* **DYNER**) — Israel's niece, Helen and Jacques's daughter.

Other Characters

DAGOBERT MEYER — Austrian opera singer and Jewish Lagerführer ("camp leader") of the Kazerne Dossin.

JACK THE MOSER (*also*, **JACK THE INFORMER, FAT JACK, GROS JACK**) — Jewish man who aided the Gestapo in tracking down suspected Jews.

JOHANNES (HANS) FRANK — Former policeman and Nazi camp commander of the Kazerne Dossin from March/April 1943 to September 1944.

JOURNÉE — Belgian Nazi described by Israel as the most violent SS officer in the Kazerne Dossin.

LUDWIG VAN KOL ("FERDE KOP" *or* **HORSE HEAD)** — Vicious Flemish SS officer in the Kazerne Dossin whose head and face resembled a horse.

MAX BODEN — Nazi commander of the Kazerne Dossin until September 1944, along with Johannes Frank.

MOSHE PATCHER (*or* **MOSHE THE SLAPPER**) — Flemish SS officer known for unexpectedly slapping people as punishment.

MR. ROSENFELD — Negotiated the Palestine Exchange List program with the Gestapo, worked with Fanny to get the Kapeluszniks on the list.

MR. TUCHMAYER (SCHMUL SELMAR TUCHMAYER) — Internee in the Kazerne Dossin who circulated information about the war to the other prisoners and SS guards.

MADAME CHRISTINE CARLIER — Madame Snyder's sister, who helped shelter the Kapeluszniks in late 1942.

MADAME SNYDER — Kapelusznik family's landlady while in hiding, who sheltered them in several different houses in Brussels.

PIERRE CARNEWAL — Belgian Resistance member who aided the Kapelusznik family in hiding

SHOLOM (SHLOMO) SILBERSHATZ (SZMUL SZULEM ZYLBERSZAC) — Fellow "Flitzer" who escaped from the infamous twentieth transport, was imprisoned with Israel.

WITH MANY MIRACLES

"Our youthful hopes of universalism and brotherly love were destroyed. The Europe we admired, respected and loved assumed strange faces."

Portrait of a Jew by Albert Memmi,
The Orion Press 1962, 5

"This building is a witness to the bestiality of the Nazis. Let's hope that the human race will defend itself more effectively against the next devil."

Israel Cappell's comments upon visiting Mechelen Concentration Camp fifty years after its liberation.

Prologue

MY GRANDCHILDREN CALL ME "Yaya." I'm not sure why, but I like the name. It seems cute and humane. The custom of calling me by that nickname began with my first grandchild, Saul, today a married man and forty-year-old parent of four. Children are sweet. Looking at it mystically, perhaps the world they come from is also sweet, so they bring all sorts of sweet and cute things with them as they travel to Earth. Saulie, as we call him in the family circle, brought this marvelous name "Yaya" as a gift for me. I love it and my other grandchildren have adopted the name too.

When they were small, my grandchildren often asked me, "Yaya, have you been to 'camp?'" I did not know how to respond. I knew what they were referring to. I had seen advertisements in places in the back section of the *New York Times Magazine* and other media, for summer camps with cheerful Native American names. Typically, young people would go in the summer months to these mountainous retreats and have a wonderful time.

I have not been to any of these idyllic spots but, sadly, I have been to what was referred to years ago as a "camp." These institutions were not advertised and had German names; fees were waived, and attendance was free, but nobody wanted to go there. These camps were year-round, not just for the summer, and attendance was compulsory (if one was Jewish). Most taken there did not return back to the earthly world as we know it. If my grandchildren ask me, "Yaya, did you learn anything in camp?" I will tell them "Yes." I learned a great deal about people, about Germans, Belgians, Jews and Christians. You, dear reader, judge for yourself whether I am correct in my conclusions.

As a man of faith, I believe that God has created a beautiful world. When I see the perfection and precision of this world . . . I am awed by its endless ingenuity. I do believe that He wanted the population of the world to participate in its creation, perhaps by finishing it. But despite the acts of kindness we were shown by strangers from time to time, the bad outweighs the good. People, I think, have generally done a miserable job in making the world a better place.

Dedication

I DEDICATE THIS MEMOIR to the people who saved my life. Dagobert Meyer, a Viennese man whom I had never met before, who was the Jewish "camp leader" of the Nazi Kazerne Dossin in Mechelen (Malines in French),* Belgium, from which some 26,000 Jews, on 28 convoys, went to Auschwitz;† the heroic Jewish Agency people behind the Palestine Exchange List,‡ including the Brussels Pales-

---

* Editors: Situated in the Dutch-speaking region of Flanders, the transit camp in which the Cappells were held is most commonly referred to in English by the name "Mechelen." The camp is also known in French as "Malines," and sometimes referred to as "Mechelen/Malines" or "Mechelen-Malines."

† Editors: The Kazerne Dossin, or the SS-Sammellager Mechelen, was a transit camp in Nazi-occupied Belgium. Beginning in 1942, Nazi overseers deported 25,274 Jewish and 354 Roma and Sinti inmates from the Kazerne Dossin to Auschwitz-Birkenau and other Nazi death and concentration camps in Eastern Europe. Cappell originally wrote that 26 convoys left Mechelen. In fact, 28 convoys journeyed from Mechelen to Auschwitz. These transports were numbered 1-26, with three additional transports labeled Z, 22a, and 22b.

‡ Editors: For more on The Palestine Exchange Lists, see in backmatter, Netty Gross, "Last Address Unknown: The Palestine Exchange Lists were responsible for saving the lives of more than 500 Jews during the Holocaust" *The Jerusalem Post*, January 6, 1995.

tine Office head Yitzhak Shaten; Benjamin Nykerk, a Dutch Jew who
had come to Belgium in the 1930s; my brother, Charles (Yechezkel)
Kapelusznik-Cappell, who risked his life by putting us on the Palestine Exchange List to begin with; and mainly, my sister, Fanny (Feigele) Finkelstein, who defied the Nazis and escaped their clutches
and valiantly succeeded in making sure we were properly processed
on the List, thereby saving me, our parents, our older brother and her
husband.

I also remember the bravery and love of my parents, Jacob Emanuel and Sarah Esther Kapelusznik-Cappell who enjoyed *arichat
yamim* [Hebrew, lit. length of days, aka a long life] and who immigrated to Forest Hills, Queens, New York, where my father founded
Congregation Beth Jacob, a well-known "survivors' *shtiebel*" with
Rabbi Yitzchak Pierkarski from Sosnowitz, Poland as its spiritual
leader; my other siblings (now gone) and their spouses: my sister,
Helen (Chaya) and [her husband] Jacques Dyner, and [my sister]
Regine (Rifka) and [her husband] Maurice (Moshe) Dyner. (The
men were brothers and the women, sisters.) Jacques Dyner, my
brother-in-law, died tragically during the so-called "death march"
from Auschwitz—so we were told, but Helen survived and remarried a kindly German Jew, Herman Frank. With her daughter, Suzanne, they immigrated to New Jersey, in the United States, where
they rebuilt their lives.

I also honor the memories and fortitude of my in-laws, Necha (Na-
talie or Netty) and Shragah Chaim Feivel (Paul) Isboutsky, who were
imprisoned in the Kazerne Dossin at an earlier period, and miraculously survived. Of our four parents, only Shragah, born 1878, lived out
his remaining years, as he dreamt, in Israel. He died in the 1950s and is
buried in Bnei Brak, a city near Tel Aviv. I did not know the Isboutskys
(or my wife) during the war years.

As always, I am deeply indebted to my wife, Eva (Avigail) Cappell [née Isboutsky, also known as Evelyn], *until 120*, also a survivor
of the Holocaust in Belgium where she was a fellow prisoner in the

Kazerne Dossin barracks (she was not there in my time).* Born and raised in Antwerp to a devout Litvak family which migrated from Poland/Russia [i.e. a Lithuanian Jewish family from the Polish borderlands of the Russian Empire], Eva was twice arrested and sent to the Kazerne, and was a witness to Nazi barbarism. As a laborer in the camp's "reception" area (*Aufnahme*) the flower of Belgian Jewry passed before her very eyes, including her parents and younger sister (whom she and her older sister, Rachel, saved) and [her] elderly maternal grandfather, R. Kalman Dimenstein, who was deported on the seventeenth transport, which left Mechelen on October 10, 1942.†

Her courageous efforts to save him too were fruitless, although she managed to unite Kalman with his youngest son (her uncle), Noah Dimenstein, on the convoy to Auschwitz. Both men perished to our knowledge—if they survived the trip to begin with. Indeed, many of our family members and friends (both in Poland and in Belgium) vanished in the killing centers in Poland. Victims in my wife's paternal family include her first cousin, Herman Isboutsky, a member of the Resistance organization known as the "Red Orchestra."‡ Herman was caught and slain (beheaded) by the Nazis in Germany. There is a grove

---

* "Until 120" is shorthand for the Yiddish *"zi zol lebn biz 120"*: she should live until 120.

† N.G.: Born in Bialystock in 1858, Kalman was a *magid shiur* [advanced Talmud instructor]. [His] son, Noah Dimenstein, was married to Rachel (née Gutowsky). She and [their] daughter, Salome ("Sally"), age 10, were deported to Auschwitz on transport no. XXI (July 31, 1943). [Their] daughter Sophie, 16, went on transport II (July 8, 1942). Archive of the Jewish Museum of Deportation and Resistance, Kazerne Dossin, Mechelen, Belgium.

‡ Die Rote Kapelle (The Red Orchestra) was the name given to a network of anti-Nazi resisters known to the Third Reich as Abwehr Section IIIF. Members of The Red Orchestra distributed anti-Nazi literature, documented atrocities of the regime, sought to aid Jews and other political opponents of Nazism in their attempts to flee Germany, and transmitted military intelligence to the Allies.

of trees in his memory in Israel, and a service for him was arranged by
my wife's brother, David.

Fortunately, Eva and Rachel (an immigrant from Antwerp to
Brooklyn in the early 1990s) outsmarted the Nazis with extraordinary luck and pluck. Eva and I met and married after the war and
lived, for a while, in Brussels, where our first daughter, Michele, was
born. I thank Eva for her support over the period when I was writing this memoir. Together, on the ashes of the past, we created a new
life. With the Almighty's help, Eva and I built a *bayit ne'eman b'yisrael* [Hebrew: a faithful home among the Jewish people] and we salute
our three children, their wonderful spouses, our eleven grandchildren
and their dear spouses and children: our oldest daughter Michele (née
Cappell) Bankhalter and her husband Alan Bankhalter; her four children, Saul and his wife, Deena (née Barth) Fiedler; Alisa (née Fiedler)
Oliner and her husband, Ari Oliner; Ilana ("Buji") (née Fiedler) Lawrence and her husband Robbie Lawrence; and Daniel ("D. J.") Fiedler;
our son, Kenny, and his wife Marcie (nee Besdine) Cappell; and their
three children Sam, Jamie, and Anna; and our daughter Netty Gross-
Horowitz (née Cappell) and Professor Elliott Horowitz; and Netty's
four children, Ayala (nee Gross) and her husband Yossie Horwitz;
Tamar (née Gross) and her husband David Friedenburg; Avi Gross
and Dani Gross.

Unlike many of our age, Eva and I had the enormous *zechut*
[Hebrew: privilege or reward] to see generations live in freedom and
with dignity. The impossible came true and we lived to tell the tale,
and that is precisely what I aim to achieve with this memoir, written
over the course of [many] years and completed in my ninetieth year.
My story is an important link in the chain that led to the decimation
of European Jewry during the Second World War.

INTRODUCTION

World War II Begins

THERE MIGHT HAVE BEEN certain advantages to living in a western country like Belgium during the Holocaust period. Some saintly Belgian non-Jews helped Jews, and the Resistance movement was active. At various times, in an effort to placate Queen Elisabeth of Belgium, the Nazis promised the Association of Belgian Jews (ABJ) that it would be allowed to maintain old-age homes and children's orphanages (from which Jews would not be poached). Sometimes their promises were kept, sometimes not. But fact is, these perks were non-existent in the East [aka Eastern Europe]—to my knowledge, and in the end, perhaps not surprisingly, approximately fifty percent of Belgian Jews are believed to have survived the Holocaust.

Still, Belgium was hardly safe, and the Shoah was not a pretty picture there. The distance between the civilized streets of Brussels or Antwerp and the horrors of Auschwitz was just a train-ride away, if one was caught. But even before the abysmal journey to Poland, the Nazis instituted systematic policies of terror, curfews, arrests, beatings, imprisonment, transit-camps, trains and [the use of] attack dogs in Belgium. In short, the experience of being Jewish during the Second

World War in Belgium was panic-filled. For every other Jew, the encounter with the Nazis was lethal.

We hid for two years in rented apartments in Brussels, running low on funds and food, until one night, we were savagely arrested by the Gestapo.* Imprisoned in the Kazerne Dossin, and a millimeter away from being deported to Auschwitz, extraordinary luck intervened in the form of the Palestine Exchange List and our presence on it (miraculously confirmed by the International Red Cross in Geneva). This documentation saved us from a terrible fate. But we came exceedingly close to being deported and my eldest sister and her husband, in fact, were. (She survived Auschwitz; he did not.) The Kazerne Dossin was the gateway to Hell.

We had no illusions. For seven years, from 1933-1940, we had witnessed the persecution of Jews in neighboring Nazi Germany. We tried to help the refugees who managed to slip through the borders into Belgium. But the Nazis became bolder in their wretched behavior and after Kristallnacht in 1938 and the doomed voyage of the St. Louis ship in 1939 (which disturbed us terribly), everything got worse.†

Plenty of Europeans and even some Americans harbored forms of anti-Semitism in those years. It was a time when people were not ashamed to show feelings of disdain for minority groups. Fact is, I grew up with anti-Semitism so I should not have been surprised. When I

---

* Aka the *Geheime Staatspolizei*, the Nazi secret police.

† Editors: "Kristallnacht," also known as the "Night of Broken Glass," refers to a night of rampant, public, anti-Jewish violence that took place on November 9-10, 1938 throughout the German Reich. Thousands of synagogues, Jewish institutions, cemeteries, and businesses were vandalized and destroyed. The St. Louis was a German ocean liner that, in May 1939, carried 937 passengers, most of them Jewish refugees fleeing Nazi Germany for Cuba (with the hope of traveling on to the United States). After their landing was denied by both the Cuban and American authorities, the passengers were obliged to return to Europe, where many perished in the Holocaust.

was a child, there was even a column in one of the local Belgian newspapers entitled "The Jewish Problem."

But the sheer dimensions of Hitler's hatred for Jews, and the wild applause he received, were new to me. When I saw the weekly news of the world at my local movie theater, the *Cinéac* in Brussels, I could not comprehend the German public's delirious reaction to Adolph Hitler. It was as if the masses were in a trance. The many thousands (maybe more) of outstretched German hands, screaming "Heil Hitler," were a frightening spectacle. Unsurprisingly, I felt that people were generally made of stone back then and, except for a few voices, I began to think that I was living in the "stone age."

The Holocaust in Belgium didn't start with bullets, pits filled with bleeding bodies and ghettos as it might have in Eastern Europe. For me, it all started calmly on the beautiful morning of May 10, 1940. A young, bookish man who had just turned eighteen, I was awoken by the thunder of anti-aircraft artillery. Sauntering out on the balcony of our apartment in Brussels, perched very high in the clear blue sky, I saw what looked like tin, silver toy planes surrounded by gray puffs emitted by anti-aircraft guns. As someone who avidly followed the news, I understood that we were facing war. Despite the beautiful morning and the "excitement" in the air, I knew that war was a dreadful event. These days, the Second World War is justifiably seen as an immense tragedy for all of humanity, especially for the Jews.

Just how terrible, animalistic, even ferocious, humans can be to one another became apparent to me (and to the world) in the years after the war, when its nightmarish toll became public. Soldiers lost their lives; Jews were tortured and murdered (including many members of my family), Roma ("gypsies") were deported to death camps or were brutally slaughtered in places like the Lodz ghetto, and blameless civilians were killed in the mayhem.

Though I survived, like many others my faith in society was shattered. I found myself wondering: what is the purpose of religion, "culture" and civil society if mankind can sink to such low depths, if the thirst for violence and bloodshed is so untamable? After all, the Germans were believed to be the most "cultured" people on Earth. The non-German collaborators with their venomous feelings for Jews were also a mystery to me. I would later encounter these people (if you can call them that) in the form of foreign SS troops (along with Belgian-Flemish soldiers) who were sympathizers of the Nazi regime.* (Milder forms of anti-Semitism among "ordinary" Belgians, which we encountered over the years, included the stealing of Jewish property post-war and/or indifference to our fears and fates during the war period.)

Indeed, on that brilliant spring morning in 1940, Hitler's military machine ignored all previous pledges and invaded three neutral countries, and I was terrified. We all were. Before World War II, there were about 65,000 to 75,000 Jews in Belgium; many of them had come in waves of immigration from Eastern Europe and some ninety-four percent were not citizens. (Nor was I a Belgian citizen.)

Though raised in Brussels, I was born in Lodz, Poland in 1922. I immigrated with my family to Belgium at age six or seven, in 1929. Today I am still fluent in the Polish language and am proud of my Polish ancestry and heritage. But I am also deeply conflicted because my beautiful native land is drenched in Jewish blood.

As a Jew, I knew what to expect upon the entry of the Nazis into Brussels, the lovely city where I grew up after my parents emigrated. Indeed, with the advance of the Nazis, my pleasant, cheerful life was about to be darkened by oncoming clouds. I only hoped that someday I would see the sunshine again. Now, we were like the persecuted "German Jews" upon whom we had once gazed with pity. Now, we Belgian Jews—citizens and non-citizens [alike]—were on the run. Soon other "enemies of the Reich" would feel the Nazi's wrathful claws.

---

* Editors: The reference is to the Flemish Legion, a Nazi collaborationist military formation made up of Dutch-speaking volunteers from German-occupied Belgium. The organization was formed in the summer of 1941; its volunteers served the SS primarily on the Eastern Front, alongside similar formations of volunteers from other parts of Nazi-occupied Europe.

Initial American reluctance to enter the war (voiced by some Jews too) was very bad for those of us stuck in Europe. Our lives hung by a hair as we desperately waited for news that an Allied fighting force had arrived. But until that happened, we were alone and unprotected and subject to Nazi laws. Jews, certainly in the eyes of the Nazis, were like a swarm of ants who had to be stamped out. In other words, we were easy prey. The ant analogy was prescient. When I was imprisoned in a Nazi camp I looked with envy at the ants. They were not Jewish and could march freely about. Nobody would beat them, and they did not have to salute the SS.

ONE

Walking to France

SO, THERE IT WAS: what we always feared might happen actually
happened. The Nazis trampled over Belgium's borders and pushed
forward. Panic engulfed the entire population, particularly the Jews.
Although we could not imagine what was in store for us, observing
what had happened in Germany we seriously considered escaping. In
truth, we had some hope in the beginning that the German military
would be contained. After the first attack, Belgium opened its borders
to French and British military forces. I saw the troops of foreign armies
passing in the street with trucks and small tanks by the thousands.*

Our hearts started beating with new hope. After all, we told ourselves that the British and the French were the giants of World War

---

* Editors: On May 10, 1940, the Third Reich attacked Belgium as part of its invasion of western Europe. British and French commanders rushed forces to the
Franco-Belgian border in an attempt to halt the German Army on that front,
resulting in weakened French defensive lines elsewhere that were easily broken
through by German tanks and infantry. The Belgian army surrendered on May
28, 1940, marking Germany's conquest of the country.

I. But as the dreadful hours went by, the news worsened. We heard that the Allied Forces were being defeated and the mood of the Jewish population in Brussels, our crowd, became increasingly worried and somber.

Jews we knew personally—such as friends, rabbis, acquaintances—had all decided to flee. Fear of living under the Nazis was palpable. The conventional thinking was that it was preferable to leave the comfort of one's home and risk the unknown rather than to stay put and allow the Nazis to dictate our fates.

We lived in a square adjacent to the railroad station. Every day, we watched as thousands of people, Jews and non-Jews, and their children, thronged toward the station, carrying bundles of belongings. We saw among them almost the entire Jewish community of Brussels pass [by] our balcony, hoping to get on trains heading toward France. The masses of non-Jewish Belgians included residents of towns and cities in French Flanders, [who were] unwilling to live under German rule.* But very few trains departed the station because the planes of the Third Reich were bombing both the roads and tracks. Still, people didn't seem to care and kept arriving in even greater numbers, sleeping in the streets.

Jews who succeeded in escaping the "trap" could not escape the "net," to paraphrase the Prophet Isaiah.† Indeed, few of those Jews who "ran" at that time escaped the Nazi dragnet as it spread its dark wings across Europe. But that was in the future. Right now, events at the present time were sufficiently awful and tragic. People who just yesterday had homes, tables and beds, became refugees and homeless overnight. Soon, panic and confusion overcame us too. The fear of con-

---

* Editors: French Flanders is the portion of the traditionally Dutch-speaking region of Flanders that is part of modern-day France.

† Editors: "And who flees from the sound of terror shall fall into the pit and who gets up from the pit shall be caught in the trap." Translation by Robert Alter, *The Hebrew Bible*, Isa. 24:18.

fronting the Nazis convinced us to run but the roads had their own hazards. There were Stukas, precision dive bombers everywhere, [I.C.: Stuka is short for the German *Sturzkampfflugzeug* which means "dive combat airplane"]. These planes were also armed with deadly machine guns. We had no beds or food or plans and wondered, *Where will we go? What shall we eat? Where should we sleep?* In addition, we didn't have enough money to last even for a week.

But our choices were limited. On the fourth day of the invasion, the German military had broken through the front lines and Third Reich soldiers were marching on Brussels. The pressure to leave was now intense. We decided to join the masses of refugees on the roads and run for our lives. Brussels was bombed several times by the Stukas, in the hope that these attacks would spread panic and prevent trains from running, which they did.

Our group was made up of Orthodox Jews, decidedly Hasidic, and consisted initially of eight adults and one newborn infant who was just four weeks old. My parents, Sara Esther (née Taub) and Jacob Kapelusznik—people in their late fifties; older brother, Charles (Yechezkel) in his twenties; sister, Regine (Rifka), and her husband, Maurice Dyner (Moishe); another sister, Fanny, (Feige) and her husband, Josef Finkelstein and me, Israel. My nephew, Henri (Avrumeleh), was the baby of Regine and Maurice Dyner.*

Before we departed on the trek to France, my father and Charles went outside to find some sort of "vehicle" which might take us there. In anticipation of seeing them, I looked out the window impatiently.

---

* I.C.: In time, the Dyners and the Kapeluszniks would have multiple marriages binding them: My older sister, Helen (Chaya) was married to Jacques Dyner; another sister, Regine, was married to his brother, Maurice; a third Dyner brother, Solomon (Shlameck), would marry a sister of Charles' second wife, Pola. Finally, Kreindel Dyner, the mother of the clan, and a daughter of Rabbi Abraham Zev Perlmutter (1844-1926), chief rabbi of Poland, and a member of the Polish *Sejm* (parliament) representing the Agudath Israel party, married my maternal uncle, Yitzchak (Icek) Taub, after both were widowed from their first spouses.

The radio was blaring news and bulletins every few minutes, all very bad as far as we were concerned. I remembered the harrowing stories which German-Jewish refugees had told us as they made their way to Belgium from Nazi Germany. Many had been to places like Dachau and Buchenwald and endured indignities and terrifying experiences such as shaved heads and broken jaws. And they were lucky to be alive! Now I belonged to *that* crowd. The comparison sent shivers down my spine, and I was anxious to run as far as possible.

My father and Charles finally arrived with the "vehicle" that was going to take us all to France. To my great astonishment, I saw a cart with a skinny horse and a man called Jan. The cart, horse and Jan were hired for 300 francs to take us to the French border. That was the best "vehicle" they could find in those circumstances. Cars and trucks were all gone, and whomever had some sort of rolling object to rent charged unaffordable (for us) prices.

But there was no more time to ponder about what would happen to us. My father announced that we were going, and he told us that we would rely on the Almighty's help. My father's deep belief was always so reassuring; it made me feel as if I had nothing to worry about anymore. Indeed, we did not know where we were going, where we would sleep or what we would eat—and we had a four-week-old baby in tow. But all my worries were gone. "The Almighty would help and somehow things will work out," announced my father. And so, we loaded the hapless cart with our most precious belongings: food, merchandise from our inventories of two businesses (silk, flowered dresses, which Charles and my father sold; and two valises filled with items from my own business[es] such as my leather wallet business.)

The war took us by surprise and all our capital was in inventory. Our combined liquid assets were just 1,100 Belgian francs, a very small sum for nine souls going out into the unknown. But I did not worry because the Almighty would help us. My father's optimistic words rang in my ears. And that is precisely what happened. It was rough going for a while, but the Almighty guided us through what amounted to fire, but we did not burn; through water, but we did not drown.* To what do I attribute these extraordinary miracles?

I always had heard that my maternal grandfather, Rabbi Israel Taub, better known as the (first) Modzhitser rebbe (himself a descendent of esteemed personalities), was a revered rebbe, a so-called *himmel-mensch* ("a man of heaven") and that my paternal grandfather, Chaim Wolf Kapelusznik, an industrialist in Lodz, was legendary for his acts of charity and piety. A pillar of Hasidic belief is that the good deeds accumulated by a parent or grandparent may benefit his or her offspring. In embarking on this arduous trip, I felt that we would have to use all the "credit" gathered by my grandparents. Little did I know that in the coming years . . . I would rely on that "account" repeatedly and earnestly.

My mother, sisters and baby nephew sat in the cart while we men walked alongside. I wondered if Jan would keep to the deal. I asked myself: how crazy does one have to be to take eight Jews and a baby from Brussels to France in the midst of a battle, on a journey that, by horse cart, may take a week, all for 300 francs? Maybe we were using up our first "credit?" But the Jan episode was not "miraculous." Neither crazy nor the prophet Elijah in disguise (as Judaism teaches about miracle-workers), Jan was simply an honest man with a human heart who kept his word scrupulously. And so, we started to walk on a journey which would take us to France. We were a pathetic sight: Jan, the skinny horse, the shaky cart with its occupants, scattered belongings and us men.

Soon our house and street disappeared from sight, and after two hours or so of walking, we were no longer traveling on familiar streets. We walked through parts of Belgium that I had never seen before. Hardly alone, the roads were clogged with huge, endless lines of refu-

---

* Editors: "Should you pass through water, I am with you, and through rivers— they shall not overwhelm you. Should you walk through fire, you shall not be singed, and flames shall not burn you." Translation by Robert Alter, *The Hebrew Bible*, Isa. 43:2.

gees. It resembled a giant demonstration against Nazism or huge protest march against the "wrongness" of the world—although we did not
yet know *how* wrong. We struck up acquaintances with other refugees
and exchanged information about the most recent movements of the
German army.

Nature, at least, was kind to us. The weather was balmy, and the
sun shone robustly. We walked by beautiful views of flowers in bloom
and the scent of spring was everywhere. The birds' chirping echoed
through the prairies and the forests as if these animals were mating.
The juxtaposition of beauty and terror brought to (my) mind Chaim
Nachman Bialik's famous Hebrew poem in which he describes a

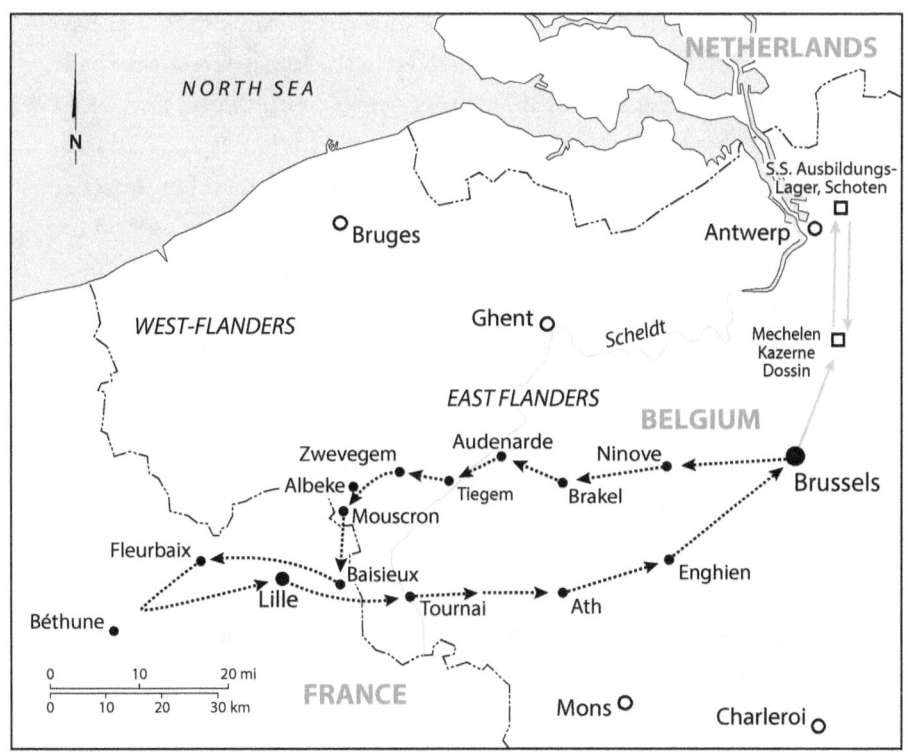

The Kapelusznik/Cappells' wartime movements

Ukrainian city after a pogrom, ". . . and God has blessed us with twins, a slaughter and a spring. The flower bloomed, the sun shone, and the slaughterer slaughtered . . . "*

We walked for twenty-two kilometers on our first day as "refugees." By nightfall, we had become quite tired and the sunny, balmy weather turned chilly. The baby, by then, was crying and we urgently started searching for a place to sleep. We arrived in a small Flemish town called Ninove and started to knock on doors. Most of the people in the homes responded from behind closed doors with lines like "we are full to capacity." But a door opened in one house in response to our knocking and a large, well-lit living room came into view. People were sitting on chairs throughout. The owner of the house was a heavy-set Flemish man with a kindly face. He approached us and said, "I have no room for anyone to sleep but if the women and child want, they can have chairs for the night and the men can sleep in the forest across the road."

We readily accepted the offer. It was close to midnight, and everybody was exhausted. The baby had been crying for hours and had to be changed, fed and put to bed. We men went to the forest. Jan detached the horse from the two-wheel cart. Some of us slept in the cart on top of our belongings and the others on the grass and weeds. The forest ground was littered with refugees and their belongings. Next to me slept a Belgian army officer who had escaped the front where most of his battalion had been killed or ran away, he said. He also said that the Belgian fortifications at Fort Eben-Emael on the Dutch border, (which took years to build), were pulverized within hours. After hearing this depressing bit of news, I turned on my side and luckily fell asleep.

I awoke early and saw hundreds of refugees stretching deep into the forest, sleeping *al fresco* all around us. Luckily, our group's "encampment" was close to the road and facing the home of our kind host. After rising, we knocked on the door of the nice Flemish man's home,

---

* Editors: The reference here is to Hayim Nahman Bialik's influential "In the City of Slaughter."

and he opened it. Graciously, he said we could use his facilities to wash and have coffee and bread and we could see that he did his best to help those in need. In the meantime, Jan re-attached the horse and put our things together. He made room on the cart for my sister, Regine, and her newborn son and we resumed our march toward France.

Our next destination was Brakel, a municipality in East Flanders, and Audenarde (or Oudenaarde in Flemish), another Flanders municipality (famous in medieval times for its tapestries). The "scene" was the same wherever we went: The magnificent weather—blue skies, sunshine and balmy air—belied the desperation of the moment. Thousands of refugees lined both sides of the road and the military traffic traveled in the middle. The Nazis, too, took advantage of the perfect visibility and ruled the skies with their Stukas while the British and the French had World War I vintage planes. Jews had good reason to flee but why did the Belgian non-Jews run? I could not quite understand it, and still don't. Suffice it to say, it was a time, I think, of great uncertainty about what might happen under German rule.

The walking became very tiresome. Fortunately, most of us were young and healthy—although the baby was emerging as a big problem. We ran out of baby formula and only with great difficulty did we manage to find regular milk and sometimes raw milk. Predictably, the baby got diarrhea and we had no medication. But he was strong and somehow weathered the crisis. Next, the baby's father, my brother-in-law, Maurice (Moishe) fell and injured himself on a dirty piece of metal. He bled and needed medical attention. We stopped a car of medics from the British military and asked for help.

I was amazed how patient and calm the British medics were. First, they asked us for identification papers and when they saw that our names were Moses, Israel, Jacob, Joseph and Ezekiel, they smiled and said, "so you are all Bible people; we will take care of you." They disinfected Maurice's wound and put on it the proper bandages but realized that they had no sling. Suddenly, one of the British medics tore part of his shirt and made a sling. I was deeply impressed that he did that.

We still had some food but started to substantially deplete our provisions. I said to myself, the Almighty will have to step into the situation soon and help prevent us from going hungry! We reached Audenarde [Oudenaarde] by nightfall and entered an abandoned farm. No one was there, only the cows braying to be milked, but we didn't know how to milk cows. We somehow arranged beds for everybody to sleep in, and being very tired, we fell soundly asleep. Jan stayed with us all the time, as promised in the agreement, and was very helpful. Early in the morning, we walked in the direction of Tiegem. Our goal was to reach France and move up north to the sea. We just wanted to stay out of the Nazis' reach. We prayed that the British and French forces would stop the German advance.

The walk was the same with masses of refugees [and] military traffic clogging the roads. Occasionally, the dive bombers would swoop low and shoot bullets, killing defenseless refugees. Perhaps the German pilots thought this was a game or sport. Soon we had our own Stuka "experience." On the third day, we were walking on a wide, paved road, under a blue sky, and suddenly, a dive bomber appeared very high. He descended rapidly at a highway crossing, and everybody ran into a café for cover. I noticed that my baby nephew was abandoned in his carriage, and I could not leave him alone. I stayed with him as the dive bomber came down right over us but refrained from dropping a bomb. He simply went back up and disappeared into the sky. I asked myself: *Had he seen us—a defenseless young man with a baby in a carriage—and decided not to bomb us, or was it a miracle?* After the plane was safely away, everybody came out of the café, and an argument ensued about why the baby was left alone. In this inhuman situation, we were still human beings.

The march continued and among the refugees, we were happy to encounter some familiar faces. One surprise was the Perle family. Meir Perle was my father's business partner for many years in Lodz, Poland. He was with his son, Leizer, and a friend (of the son) named Shloime Morgenstern. [Being] Hasidic Jews from the Ger sect, they soon happily joined our group. Like us, they had very little money. Actually, there was no need for much; the abandoned houses we encountered served as "hostels."

In Tiegem, we again found an abandoned farm with plenty of cheese, eggs and jam, and we slept well during the night. We rose early, prayed and continued walking, hoping to reach the next evening and crossing into France at Mouscron, a Walloon city and municipality in the Belgian province of Hainaut and then, according to our plan, we would take the train to Paris.

Only, the walking became more troublesome than expected. The women were exhausted and the baby again had diarrhea because the milk had not been boiled. In short, everything became a huge problem, and we needed a place to rest, get warm food, and [find] good beds.

In the meantime, we arrived in the town of Zwevegem—12 people now, and a baby—and we looked for an abandoned farm as we had done in the past. But because we were exhausted, and hungry for warm food, we simply knocked on a door and out came an older man of medium height with eyeglasses. He looked at this dilapidated, desperate group of Jews and understood the situation. We did not have to open our mouths to explain. Come in people, come in, he said in French. *"Faites comme chez vous"* ("Make yourself at home") he said repeatedly. His wife came in to greet us and the hospitality extended to us was indescribably gracious. Turns out, our host and his wife were deeply religious Catholics and knew the Bible well. They apparently found in us an opportunity to do *"mitzvot"* (good deeds).

I was so impressed with the boundless goodness of this unnamed couple that I will never forget them. They gave my parents their own bedroom; they gave each of us fresh, comfortable beds; conscious of our adherence to the laws of *kashrut* (dietary laws), they set a table with food that we could eat (bread, butter, cheeses, eggs, apples, pears and plums); and they boiled fresh milk for the baby. This stay and the much-needed rest it afforded was a life saver for each of us. They did everything to make us comfortable and please us. We stayed for two nights.

In the morning of our final day, it was time to go. In a discussion amongst ourselves, we compared our host, favorably, to our Uncle Reuven, the brother of our paternal grandfather, Chaim Wolf of Lodz. Both men were known to have performed many good deeds and earned fame for their hospitality. Jan, as always, was ready for the march and wanted to finish his job. We were now heading for other towns on our itinerary, including Albeke.

As we trudged on, every day was the same, . . . the endless walking, the masses of refugees, the Stukas, the unhappy baby, and the problems. We passed Albeke and reached the border town of Mouscron. The crucial moment had arrived for Jan. He removed all the luggage from the cart and received his 300 francs and wished us goodbye. All of a sudden, our situation was *very different* than it had been before. We no longer had a cart and a horse. We retreated to another vacant farm. There, my brother, brother-in-law (Maurice), and Leizer, went out to find a pushcart (wheelbarrow) to replace Jan's. The plan was that we would take turns being the "horse."

They came back with a large farmer's cart which they found. We loaded it and *en avant* the caravan was on its way to the town (today a city) of Baisieux, located in northern France, in the district of Lille. We arrived in the late afternoon and [ended] up in an abandoned and almost empty farm. In fact, the entire village was devoid of people and scary. We still had plenty of food from "Uncle Reuven," who made sure that we had provisions for our journey and gave us a lot of cheese as well as 150 hardboiled eggs which he placed in a huge basket. That food kept us going for quite a while.

We managed to arrange places to sleep for everybody, said our evening prayers, and slept. The doors were open—there were no locks, and all farms seemed to be dilapidated and dusty as though they had been uninhabited for some time. But we were too tired to speculate. Only this time, the sound of heavy artillery awoke us from our slumber. At first the noise sounded far away but it was getting closer. We did not know the situation on the front, and we had no radio or newspapers to inform us, only hearsay from the other refugees.

The front was fast approaching us. Our destination was the French town of Béthune. We passed another abandoned farm on that hot day and sought—but could not find—anything to drink. We stopped at another farm where, once again, we encountered cows which desperately needed to be milked. Leizer Perle claimed that he knew how to milk cows and because we had no clean glasses or cups, he squirted the milk straight into our parched mouths with everyone taking a turn. We took milk for the baby who later developed green diarrhea from the "meal."

We finally reached the outskirts of Fleurbaix, a farming village some fifteen miles (24 kilometers) southeast of Béthune, where we had a rather disconcerting incident involving our merchandise—dresses, blouses, handbags and wallets—which we had piled in the cart. Passing through the main street of Fleurbaix, someone reported to the French police authorities that we might be looters. Having seen three bearded men (my father, Meir Perle and Shloime Morgenstern), the "reporter" decided that the Jews had come to make trouble.

Taken to the police station, the gendarmes inspected the valises and agreed that the evidence suggested that we had been looting—a very serious accusation. Fact is, fleeing the Germans and not knowing when, if ever, we might return, we grabbed whatever merchandise we could. But go explain that during a war! It was a very difficult situation which my brother, Charles, saved by some miracle. Asking to speak to the captain of the police station, he remained calm. In came a graying Frenchman with silvery hair and a humane expression on his face. Trembling, my brother launched into a speech that brought the captain to tears. Charles, developing confidence as he spoke, explained that we were Jews escaping the Germans, walking from Brussels with women and a baby. "What else do you want from our poor lives?" he finally asked poignantly.

The captain was very touched and offered us "anything I have here that can help you." He offered us bread, water and Martel, a brand of cognac. He said (I assume with regard to the German occupation), "We are all in big trouble. Go on your way and may God protect you.

I am sorry for all the aggravation this might have caused you. Please forgive me."

We organized our motley crew and, exhausted, continued the march to Béthune. Thinking back, it's miraculous that no one fell apart from exhaustion or malnourishment on our long journey. We rejoined a long line of refugees walking on the side of the main road. The weather continued to be clear, offering the Luftwaffe no resistance and total domination of the skies. One could tell that they had prepared well for war. Once again, by evening, we found an abandoned farmhouse with broken doors and windows. Practically devoid of furniture, we improvised places to sleep but were (again) awoken in the night by the sounds of heavy artillery which approached us.

TWO

Bathing in Cognac in Lille, France

AS THE HOURS ADVANCED, we saw refugees going in the opposite direction, back to Belgium. We stopped some people and asked them why they were returning. The road to Béthune was littered with dead bodies, they said. The Stukas are machine-gunning the refugees. Cut off and encircled by the Germans, the British and the French defense forces seemed *kaput*. Free passage along the roads was no longer a possibility. There was no escape, we were told, and it was useless, not to mention very risky to continue. The only open route was to go back. That is what we heard over and over again from all the returnees.

Among the "returnees" was a group of kind-hearted French Sephardim who were somehow surprised to meet Belgian Jews. Sympathetic toward us, they said they were from Lille, a large city in northern France (French Flanders). They suggested to us we should go there too because we would find "Yiddish, Torah and even a *shnorer*."* Of

---

* Editors: A *shnorer* is a Yiddish term for a beggar or moocher. The term carries a negative connotation and is often used as an insult.

course, what they meant to say was that there was a Jewish community in Lille, which, theoretically, might help us. One man in their group gave us his address and told us that we should come to his shop, and he offered to give us fresh underwear and diapers for the baby.

Touched by their kindness, we followed them on the road to Lille, arriving on Friday [at] midday. Stopping in a public park, we decided that some of the men in our party would go to the center of town and see what kind of accommodations were available. The French and British militaries were resisting the German onslaught and there were a lot of sirens announcing the latest wave of attacks. In the meantime, the men who went foraging for accommodations came back with good news: British soldiers had detonated explosive devices and removed the locks on all the big hotels which were located on the Place de la Gare, (the main railway station.) We were assigned rooms on the second and fourth floors of the Hôtel de Flandres.

Upon hearing this news, our "caravan" immediately left the park and proceeded with the hand truck to the Place de la Gare and entered the Hôtel de Flandres. A miracle unfolded before our eyes, and it was as though we entered some sort of paradise. At [a] breaking point after so many days of walking, we now had normal—and beautiful—rooms with showers and tables and chairs and normal beds. All of the hotels were now occupied by refugees. The problems were that we had no food, and the siren wailed all the time. We were told that 100,000 British and French troops were trying to defend Lille, and this sounded encouraging.

We parked the pushcart in a garage across the street and made plans for a prolonged stay. The military ordered the bakeries to open, and other food became available in newly re-opened stores. We managed to have some kind of Shabbat meal since it was Friday night after all.

We had no wine, but the cellar of the hotel was full of Scotch, Martel cognac and cases of cologne. There was electricity; the elevators were running and there was water. (All this changed later on.) It was the most comfortable time since we left our home in Brussels.

We managed to get several cozy, clean rooms with plump hotel beds. I recall that my room was in the front with a terrace literally facing La Place de la Gare. Very exhausted, we all went to sleep for the first time in some kind of comfort. The roar of artillery fire was going on all night but, tellingly, it had little effect on our sleep.

Saturday morning, my father, brother, and one brother-in-law ventured out to find a synagogue. Surprisingly, they found religious services and met the Sephardi man we had encountered on our way to Lille. He invited them to his home for *kiddush* [blessing over the wine] and repeated his offer to go to his shop on Sunday and get all the linen and underwear we needed. Those of us that stayed behind in the hotel rested [and] decided that in these circumstances Martel cognac was kosher, and we made a number of *lekhayims* [toasts to good health].

The Sabbath passed uneventfully and on Sunday the first task was to join a long queue in the morning at an open bakery and to get one large, round bread per person which we would eat with jam that we found in jars in the cellar of the hotel. There was nothing else to eat and we were very happy to have at least *something* to satisfy our hunger. Luckily, we also found cans of powdered milk in the cellar for the baby and ourselves.

But standing in line for the bread was risky because as soon as a crowd would assemble, the sirens would wail, and everybody would run for shelter. The German planes would toss a few bombs to terrorize the population and then disappear. Somehow, I was not afraid of the bombs and remained in the queue. On one unforgettable (to me) morning, after a few moments the siren wailed in a single long blast to signal the end of the bombing. When the people came back to the queue, I was delighted to be the first, and got my precious bread right away.

Sitting in the front room, with the balcony on La Place de la Gare, there was a knock at the door. *Who could that be*, we wondered? There was no hotel "service." Opening the door gingerly, we were surprised to see two German soldiers. They told us in broken French that they would like to install communication wires on the balcony. We were pleasantly surprised that they were polite and did not make any slurs or comments about Jews. After they did their job on the balcony, they smiled, waved and bade us "Auf Wiedersehen." Maybe the Germans weren't so bad, we said among ourselves. (Later, however, we had many experiences with the Nazis, who showed us how sadistic and brutal they really were.)

Shortly before the Nazis entered Lille, all water and electricity was cut off and we washed ourselves with beer and Martel cognac which we found in abundance in the cellar. We were never short on food of one kind or another. Two Jewish "characters" materialized in the hotel. One of them claimed that his name was Mr. Tennenbaum and that he was a descendent of the Tshortkever [Chortkov/Czortków] *rebbe*. Later, we learned from them that they were escaped criminals from a jail in Lille. But they were very friendly to us—like family—and our association with them came in very handy. For example, when food ceased to be plentiful, they somehow always managed to provide something to eat at a moment's notice. Nevertheless, our suspicions about their "ethics" grew and we tried to distance ourselves from them (even [though] there was nothing to steal from us.)

Besides those already described in our ever-expanding group were two people I haven't yet mentioned: a refined, elderly Jew from Vienna with a white beard, and his wife. The man's name was Rabbi Osher [Asher] Horowitz and we nicknamed him the "sweet soul." We had met the rabbi and his wife in Tournai (Belgium) on our walk to France. Like my parents, they were Hasidic. Unfortunately, they had nothing materially to contribute to the group such as money, a car, special skills or even a pushcart—but just themselves and that, too, was problematic. Rabbi Horowitz's snowy white beard was like a red scarf to a bull as far as the Nazis were concerned.

Several days passed by in Lille, and these days had a rhythm of their own. During the daylight hours, we heard bombardments and at night we heard the noise of artillery from a distance. Hampering our decision-making process was the complete news black-out. There were no newspapers and . . . no radio. One day, the lights and water went out, and life in the hotel was not as idyllic as we once thought. In fact, life became quite problematic. The toilets filled rapidly with human waste and could not be flushed, and we were only able to wash ourselves with Martel cognac.

The next day the streets emptied and watching events from the balcony became the only way we could figure out what was going on. We understood from the movements below that the Germans were about to enter the city. Shortly after breakfast, that is exactly what happened. The Nazi entry into Lille seemed sudden. First, patrol units appeared on motorcycles with machine guns on La Place de la Gare right in front of us, and for the first time in my life I saw Nazi soldiers in their *feldgrau* uniforms ("field gray" was the color of the field uniform of the German army from late 1907 until 1945; before that it was blue). Then came large tanks, a size which we had never previously seen. What is going to happen to us now, we wondered?

THREE

Back to Brussels

WE DECIDED TO LEAVE Lille and go back to Brussels. Lille was now officially occupied, and we had no reason to stay. The Nazis did not act with any particular hostility toward the Jews, and we barely knew about the Gestapo.* I later learned that as part of their propaganda campaign, the soldiers were ordered, upon their arrival, to be friendly to the population in Western countries; the opposite of their strategy in the East. The feeling was that they wanted to make a good impression (at least initially) and win over the local population.

We assembled our belongings and got the pushcart which was garaged across the street, and the next day our Hasidic "caravan" started out back to Brussels on foot. The baby continued to be a source of ongoing problems. He was very cranky, and we had no baby food of any kind. He was drinking raw milk and his carriage broke down.

---

* [I.C.: short for *Geheime Staatspolizei* (Secret State Police) of Nazi Germany, which was first under the administration of Chief of German Police, Heinrich Himmler]

We entered an abandoned furniture store and found a crib on wheels which would serve as a baby carriage. But it was difficult to pacify him because the crib had no shock absorbers and pushing it undoubtedly caused him to feel the many bumps on the uneven road.

As we were leaving Lille, we experienced our first encounter with Nazi anti-Semitism. Upon seeing us, a visibly Jewish group, a German soldier screamed, *"Juden fahren noch Jerusalem"* ("Jews go back to Jerusalem"). While that outburst was not so bad, it was only the beginning. Our involvement with the Nazis evolved from "sad" to "dangerous" to "life-threatening." We started on our first stretch back to our homes in Brussels. The weather continued to be glorious. We knew that the Nazis were not going to treat us Jews with "kid gloves" but none of us could imagine what was in store for us, and the rest of European Jewry.

Again, the roads were crowded with thousands of refugees, French and Belgian, walking back to their homes, with German military traffic going in both directions. The Germans were polite and correct. These front-line troops had no instructions about persecuting or killing Jews. (That was true up to a point.)

Our goal here was to reach the Belgian city of Tournai before nightfall. It was feasible despite the fact that the wheels of Henri-Avrumeleh's crib came off and had to be abandoned. Besides that, the "caravan" and the pushcart were holding up well. The baby was placed on the pushcart, and he was quieter. In Lille, we had discovered some powdered milk and a kind-hearted farmer had given us some boiled water to mix it with. We still had some food from the hotel in Lille as well as a case of Martel cognac which was particularly appreciated by my brother-in-law Josef, who treated himself to a drink straight from the bottle every few kilometers.

The "walk" was long and uneventful and our entire caravan reached a suburb of Tournai by nightfall. We sauntered into a nice neighborhood which boasted tree-lined streets with elegant, private houses. At first, we didn't dare "invade" these obviously occupied and forbidding homes but soon we had no choice. Beset with the "usual" problems and with night falling, and exhaustion overtaking us (the baby was crying to boot), we summoned the courage and rang the bell at one house. A blonde, Belgian woman opened the door. We told her that we were refugees from Brussels on our way home. She looked compassionately at us: what she saw were Jews with and without beards, elderly folk, and a newborn baby. Kind and good-hearted, she felt compelled to help us.

She told us that the house next door, a mansion, was till that very morning the headquarters of several German military generals who appeared to be in command. They had left and gave her the keys. The house was fully stocked with food and even had a well, she said, and there was a supply of wine and liquor in the cellar and a large amount of fruit preserves in glass jars. It was safe for all of us to stay there for the night, she asserted, but we had to leave early in the morning just in case the German generals returned. Such a situation, she warned, might prove very unpleasant for us and her. Of course, we accepted her kind offer and the gates were opened. In rolled the pushcart followed by our motley crew.

The interior of the house was intoxicatingly rich with beautiful furnishings and artwork. It did not take long, and we inspected the cellar with all the goodies. Scotch and cognac were soon flowing and the jars of preserves emptied quickly. The house was still crammed with German newspapers and maps of military operations. We became particularly alarmed when we saw letterheads with the letters "OKW" printed on top, which stood for *Oberkommando der Werhmacht* [High Commander of the German armed forces]. We washed, ate, and prayed and fell, exhausted, on the plush couches in the rooms and on the beds in the bedrooms.

The next morning, we woke very early, perhaps at 6:00a.m., and soon our group plus the pushcart were out the front gates of the house as promised to the kindly, blonde neighbor. We were on our way to the town of Ath, a Belgian town known as the "city of giants," located in the Walloon province of Hainaut, and some twenty-five kilometers away. This time Liezer, the young Gur [Ger] Hasid and I were wheeling the pushcart. Our group was walking on a sidewalk, a slight distance from us.

Unexpectedly, we were stopped by a helmeted German military policeman (*Feldgendarme*) who inquired as to the contents on or inside the cart. "You are Jews, aren't you?" said the officer hotly, as he dismounted his motorcycle. My heart started racing wildly, I had a feeling this might end badly. The cop inspected the contents of the car and erupted in screams as only the Nazis were capable of. "You Jews have looted stores. Do you know what we do with looters? We shoot them. Follow me to the *Kommandantur* (command headquarters): there it will be decided what to do with you," said the Nazi.

The rest of the members of our group watched the scene, horrified, but exercised great emotional restraint by not interfering or following us inside the *Kommandantur*. The distance was not too long; we left the pushcart in front of the building and the policeman escorted us inside.

We waited for what seemed like an eternity, and I felt faint from nerves. Soon the commanding officer came in and lucky for us, he was a young Wehrmacht [army] major and not a member of the despised and dangerous SS. The arresting officer, bristling with anti-Semitism, reported to the major that we were Jews (as though that was a crime!) with looted materials "which I caught," he said proudly. In response to these accusations, the major asked us what was in the bags on the pushcart, and I babbled nervously in part German, part Yiddish, that the "loot" was actually our merchandise which we took with us when we escaped from Brussels. I explained to the major that we took goods and materials from our businesses in case we needed more money.

Fortunately, and extraordinarily, the major chose to believe me, not the Nazi, and dismissed the (unpleasant) cop who was sure he had caught some important criminals. The major had one last caveat: he told us to stay on the side of the road [so] as not to disturb the military traffic. "And now you are free to go to Brussels," he concluded. I was happily shocked. In fact, we were very lucky and like two men plucked from the jaws of a lion, we scrammed out of the German compound quickly, grabbed the pushcart, and ran.

The decision to take the merchandise was intended to provide us with capital but in the meantime it had brought us nothing but trouble, and we joined the rest of the family members who were waiting nearby anxiously. Everyone embraced us and I was extremely relieved to say the least.

The weather continued to be splendid which had the dual effect of allowing us to walk while also assisting the Germans with visibility. But the group began to disintegrate. My brother-in-law Josef became depressed and announced that he was unable to walk further and said he wanted to die right there; the older people, not surprisingly, walked very slowly; finally, we were all affected by the warm weather and the lack of shade from the searing sun.

Suddenly, in our desperation, another miracle came our way. An empty bus was approaching, and we raised our hands in an effort to flag it down. The bus came to a halt. It was an empty Swiss bus, and the driver told us that he was on his way to Brussels to pick up stranded Swiss citizens. A pitiful sight, he agreed to take us all back to Brussels, but he would not take the pushcart or its contents, nor (on the bright side) would he take any payment. The group agreed at once and filed quickly onto the bus all except my brother, brother-in-law Maurice, and myself.

We stayed behind to push the cart. By nightfall, we reached Ath. In need of a place to sleep, we knocked on a farmer's door. A man with a white beard opened and we told him the truth—that we were refugees returning to Brussels and that we needed a place to sleep. Alone, he was a little apprehensive at first to let in three bedraggled men. Then he said, "You are Israelites, aren't you?" We said we were, and he changed his tune and enthusiastically invited us in. In retrospect, it's amazing how being Jewish was both a positive and a negative factor in our survival. To the Nazis, it was a reason to murder us; to some religious Belgians who read the Old Testament, however, it was a blessing.

The man invited us to sit down with him in his dining room where [he] offered food and coffee and he started to talk. He told us that he was a professor at the Université libre de Bruxelles (ULB)—the Free

University of Brussels—and was a friend of Leon Kubowitzki, a leader of the Jewish community in Belgium, whom we had known too. As soon as he said this, we felt more comfortable, conversed for hours and felt like equals. He offered us the barn for sleeping and we slept on piles of straw. He related to us that he had been to Brussels and that everything seemed "normal" and that the Jews didn't suffer unusually. (This "normalcy" was short-lived. Persecuting, hunting, and incarcerating Jews was yet to come.) In the morning, our professor served us breakfast and we parted as friends.

Our next destination was the town of Enghien, some 25 kilometers away and about ten miles from Brussels. We were told that some ten kilometers from Enghien was the small town of Hal, (also known as Halle) which had a tramway going to Brussels. The walk to Enghien was easy for us. The "bus" group was surely home by now, we imagined. To our happy surprise, we discovered that the tramway to Brussels was leaving from Enghien and that we did not have to walk to Hal [Halle].

We arrived at Enghien in the early afternoon, and we removed all the luggage from the cart and re-packed it so it would fit on the tramway platform. We gave our precious pushcart to a fruit vendor who set up shop. Echoing the thoughts of the professor, everything seemed "normal" to us too. The tramway terminal was quite empty but the tram itself became fuller and fuller as we traveled along. Indeed, people were tentatively returning to their former lives and were hoping that the German occupiers would be decent and fair.

But upon reaching Brussels we had mixed feelings, weighing the harsh Nazi reality against our illusory hopes for the future. We knew, ever since 1933, when they came on the scene, that the Nazis were vicious anti-Semites and that life for the Jews there [i.e. in Germany] was exceedingly difficult with them in charge. Indeed, we had fled Brussels to save ourselves from Nazi persecution! Now, we were placing ourselves back into their hands and the unknown. Complicating our self-doubts was an aching desire to go home to our own beds, chairs, pots and pans and to have a permanent roof over our heads. We could no longer wander around like wild people.

Now that we were going back, we had a few immediate concerns. Did we still have an apartment? How would daily life be under the Nazis? These were our musings at the time. Who could be such dark prophets and predict that the Nazis had incredibly grisly and gruesome plans, and intended to assemble us in "concentration camps" and to annihilate us—the Jews of Europe? We could not imagine such a thing.

The tram seemed interminably slow, but we finally reached our stop. Our apartment (1 Rue de l'Argonne) was just around the corner. When the tram came to a halt, it took us extra time to unload all the luggage. On the sidewalk, an acquaintance named Berish Dichstein happened to pass by. Anxious to hear what was happening after our three-week absence, Berish gave us an upbeat report. He said that life was fine, business was brisk, and the Germans behaved very correctly and did not molest the Jews.

On cue, my brother returned with a big smile on his face: our parents were in the apartment, he told me, everything was still there, and nothing was removed or missing. He suggested that we take all our luggage upstairs to the apartment. And that's what we did. What a thrilling experience it was for me to open the door of our apartment after wandering on the roads, sleeping in abandoned houses and barns, and being dependent on the "kindness of strangers" with the sound of heavy artillery in the background. What a pleasure it was to sit down on one's own table and chair, and sleep in one's own bed. (But the homey feeling was temporary. By the summer of 1942, we would be gone.)

But for some our arrival was not exactly a blessing. Our landlord, a good-looking middle-aged man who wished us well when we departed for France (and gave us a case of sardines which came in handy), and his pretty, blonde wife (an anti-Semitic type) both seemed very surprised—even disappointed—when we returned but didn't say anything. We were anxious not to antagonize the man because he owned a sizable garage and repair shop which had filled up with German military cars for repair. Business was robust (for him) and Nazi officers were walking in and out of the building in which we lived.

So far, the landlord, also correct, kept to his business and did not ask us to move. We were only too happy to sleep in our beds, and to maintain a low profile. Incidentally, my married sisters and their husbands also found their homes untouched and everything precisely the way they left it. (This changed later on and there was wide-scale looting of Jewish property.)

In truth, our hearts were full of fear, and we were overwhelmed by anxiety about what might happen. We could not ignore what we knew. We knew the Nazis spelled trouble for Jews, and we were unsure of what tomorrow might bring. We knew, certainly my parents knew, that Nazi ghettos already existed in Lodz and Warsaw—their hometowns—because my father was corresponding with his friends and relatives stuck there. And we had heard dreadful stories from Jewish refugees from Germany, about Jews who had been kidnapped in the streets by SS hooligans and sent to places like Dachau and Buchenwald, where after months of beatings and ill treatment, [they] died, their ashes sent home in a box by mail. (Later on, even this "gesture" was abandoned.)

It was hardly a surprise, then, that Jews felt that they had to escape. After the war, I met some well-to-do Belgian Jews who actually succeeded in reaching the French-unoccupied zone or Spain, Portugal or Morocco. However, as I mentioned earlier, most—like us—did not succeed in crossing to freedom because the Germans were advancing faster than us.

[Editors' Note: For clarity's sake, the following two paragraphs have been moved to allow for a clear conclusion to this episode.]

My father, back a day earlier, bought some food and we ate and went to sleep, exhausted from all we had been through in the past three weeks. The next morning, I went out on the balcony which overlooked the streets leading to the main artery to France. The roads were clogged with German military vehicles which were marked with swastikas. This vehicular array including gray trucks, motorcycles, cars and tanks was impressive, but every swastika invoked in me a deep fear and sense of dread like seeing the teeth of a cannibal or monster.

(Postscript from our "walk": The Perle family survived the war years, but I am less optimistic about the fates of Shloime Morgenstern and the bearded Viennese rabbi (and his wife) whom we called the "*zise neshome*" [Yiddish: sweet soul].)

FOUR

The German Jewish Refugees of the Pre-Occupation Period

[Editors' Note: In this chapter, Israel flashes back to 1938 and the pre-occupation period in Belgium, describing his encounters with German Jewish refugees two years before the Belgian army was defeated by the Third Reich.]

THE PLIGHT OF THE German Jewish refugees was a long and heart-breaking chapter. It underscored our own vulnerability under the Nazi regime. German Jews flocked to Belgium's borders by the thousands and sometimes they were turned back—even after reaching Antwerp or Brussels—to face the Nazis. However, it did happen, occasionally, that individual Belgian police guarding the border would not bother the refugees, and would tell them when to catch a train to Brussels or Antwerp. The cops understood the plight of these people and their emotions were with the forsaken men, women and children. Generally, the Belgian people had more courage than their government, I observed.

Some of the German refugees came with financial means and were able, after a period of waiting to obtain visas, to travel to the United

States. This is what happened to the family of my friend, Erik Goldsmith, who waited with his family in Belgium for a few years and came back in 1944 as a United States army sergeant.* However, the vast majority of escaping refugees did not have the kind of money that Erik's family had.

Funds did make a difference at that stage. Certain countries allowed people to immigrate if they had the financial means to support themselves or some special skills desired by the host country. Alternatively, these countries could make immigration very difficult if the individual did not have means or skills. My impression was—and is—that there was a world-wide failure to understand how urgent it was for Jews to get out of Europe, and that there was a death warrant for all European Jews.

The images of long lines of German Jews outside various embassies are legendary. When the persecutions reached their height, thousands of German Jews could no longer wait for the bureaucracies and simply streamed illegally into Belgium, many, by their telling, stripped of their assets by brutal, marauding gangs of Nazi SAs—paramilitary "brownshirts." (SA was short for *Sturmabteilung* or Storm Detachment).

The Jewish communities of Antwerp and Brussels did their utmost to help these people by finding them apartments and organizing kitchens where they could get free meals and minimal cash subsidies. They were also helped by the American Joint Distribution Committee (JDC). But the scene was tragic.

In 1938, I met refugees from Germany named Sibetzhener and Keller, men in their forties or fifties.† Both men had escaped from Cologne (or Koln) in North Rhine-Westphalia, Germany, to Brussels with their young children. They lived in two attic rooms without heat

---

* I.C.: Sadly, he was killed in Germany days before the end of the war. The consolation for his family was that Erik died as a free Jew, a United States soldier, and not as a shivering, naked, victim in a gas chamber.

† I.C.: Their wives eventually made it to Brussels.

or water because that is all they could afford with the meager stipend from the JDC. Sibetzhener's wife and baby boy were waiting in Cologne for money to pay a smuggler to cross into Belgium.

One day, Sibetzhener approached me and asked for a favor. His baby son, who was six months old, had arrived from Germany to a smuggler's "depot" in Antwerp. Since he had no money for the train ride, and heard that I had a monthly train pass (to Antwerp), he asked me whether I could fetch the baby. It was not an easy task for a then 16-year-old boy with zero experience with babies. However, I could not refuse him and accepted the task. After a day's work, in the evening, I boarded a train to Antwerp and then took a trolley to Rolwagen Street [Rolwagenstraat] in the Jewish quarter.

An apartment on the third floor was apparently the "depot" for smuggled Jewish children from Germany including this baby. The man, a Jew, who smuggled people for financial gain, asked me which child I had come for, and I told him the Sibetzhener baby. There was a roomful of babies and children and he brought me the cute but frightened six-month-old baby wrapped in a woolen cover—it was wintertime. "Young man, you are now in charge of bringing this baby to his father who will be waiting in the Gare du Nord in Brussels."

Till then, I had never held a baby before, and I had no idea what to do if he became cranky or started to cry or throw up. It was late in the evening, and I walked down the stairs of the apartment house and I reproached myself for undertaking such a risky and difficult task, one which I found to be overwhelming. But there was no way to retreat now. I boarded the trolley car to the central train station and tried to "get to know" my new six-month-old friend. I boarded the train, sat down, and used all my ingenuity to keep the baby happy but he was fidgety. I was terrorized by the fear he inspired. What if he gets even nastier and screams? I gave him a bottle and tried to keep him as calm as I could.

Soon a heavy-set man with huge packages sat down facing me. I concluded that he was probably a Jewish merchant returning home from a market somewhere near Antwerp. He was sitting across from me and had a sympathetic face. Many Jews at that time fed their families by selling goods at public markets all over the country. It was not an easy living; everyday, before dawn, the merchants left Brussels by train to different towns with huge bundles of goods. They stood and waited for customers at rented tables until late in the afternoon. Then they would pack up their unsold "goods" and take the train back home, again lugging their heavy bundles.

Additionally, their lives were made difficult by the requirement of the state to obtain special permits because few were citizens. The permit was costly and difficult to obtain due to bureaucratic obstacles. I decided that my "neighbor" on the train was one of those merchants, tired and on his way back home. Suddenly, the baby started crying inconsolably, after all he must have been exhausted from a long trip from Germany, and who knew in what conditions he was smuggled to Belgium?

The merchant looked questioningly at me and the wailing baby—which I could not control—and asked me what I was doing late in the evening with this unfortunate child. I told him the story and he said, "Give me the baby, you are too young to have experience." To my enormous relief he took the baby from my arms and sat down and cuddled the infant until the latter fell asleep. Alas, the merchant understood the tragedy of it all and broke into mournful weeping as he cuddled the sweet, innocent victim of Nazism.

The train arrived at the Gare du Nord in Brussels, and I took back little Sibetzehener, and the merchant took his huge bundles. We walked together to the exit where Sibetzehner was waiting for his son. I handed him over and was relieved to have accomplished my mission. Sibetzehner thanked me and I, in turn, thanked the kindly merchant with a warm handshake and a brotherly hug. We all separated in the dark night, each on our own way home—or so I thought. The bus which I boarded, circled the square in front of the Gare du Nord and looking out the window, I suddenly noticed Sibetzehener, weeping forlornly on a bench in the square holding his whimpering son. It was 11:00p.m. The bus moved south towards my home, and I was very disturbed by what I had just seen. It just underscored how alone and neglected the German Jews were.

A few days later, I was approached by Keller: *Could I pick up his daughter at the same address in Antwerp?* She, too, had arrived, after having been smuggled from Nazi Germany. This was a whole different case. Keller's daughter was a twelve-year-old deaf girl who was also unable to speak. Again, I could not refuse, and on a Sunday morning, I boarded the train to Antwerp and sought out the same apartment with the same smuggler. The girl was indeed deaf and mute but despite her handicap, she was sweet, highly intelligent and pretty, with long blonde hair and beautiful eyes. She understood everything about her odyssey and could read lips and created no problems. Nevertheless, just to make sure she was happy before the trip, I took her to a shop and bought her a large packet of Belgian chocolate for which she was very grateful. Like in the other case, her father waited upon arrival in Brussels, and they [were] happily reunited.

Keller and Sibetzhener were Orthodox Jews and since they were not permitted to work, they spent their time in the study room (*beit midrash*) of the synagogue in the Anderlecht section of Brussels.*

---

* I.C.: Their efforts to save themselves and their families were courageous, but I have no idea whether either man or their wives and children survived. [Editors: The fate of Keller, Sibetzhener, and their families remains unknown.]

FIVE

Return to "Normal" (1940)

[Editors' Note: Here Israel continues to narrate his family's life under German occupation, after returning home from their unsuccessful escape to France.]

BRUSSELS STARTED TO "NORMALIZE." Persecutions against the Jews were initially non-existent although life under the German occupation was sad and filled with anxiety. (In Belgium, trouble for the Jews would only begin a year after the Nazis took over.) Back in 1940, our impression was that the Germans were too drunk with their victorious wins to open a new war against the Jews in Belgium. Stores were open and appeared to be doing well. German soldiers bought items they hadn't seen for sale back home in years. General Alexander von Falkenhausen (1878–1966) was named head of the military government of Belgium and northern France and he set himself up in a confiscated mansion in Brussels. In my understanding of the situation, he was in no hurry to impose restrictions on Jews.

Scholars of the period write that the Nazis were slow to persecute the Jews, initially, because they were keen to maintain a "human" face as a method to win over Belgian non-Jews. They also, I believe, wanted Jews to remain calm and unsuspecting, so when the summons for deportation would come, the Jews would go willingly. Deception, I learned, was a very important factor in implementing the "Final Solution." Few Jews, certainly not us, realized back then that the Nazis had in mind to kill us all.

Indeed, at the beginning of 1940, a false feeling of security developed. *Maybe they will not persecute Jews in the occupied Western countries like Holland, Belgium and France*, it was thought. Jews sensed that it was "safe" to come back to Brussels from havens they succeeded in reaching, such as southern France: and scholars say about 25,000 did return.

The "illusion" that we were safe went on for about one year, as I mentioned. Synagogues were open on Saturdays in Brussels (until October of 1941) and we went to a *shul* on Rue de la Clinique where services were quite well attended. Indeed, till the end of 1941, life for Jews was more than bearable. People made a "living" and they went about their business. Food (scarce in the stores but abundant on the black market) was available for a price and kosher meat was also to be had. There were functioning Jewish communities in Antwerp and Brussels and Jewish youth organizations were gathering for programs and discussions. Engagements and weddings were celebrated.

Reflecting the air of normalcy, we moved to a better apartment. And we even bought a new Philips radio which had short wave reception capabilities. I could listen to American radio and that authoritative voice from New York still rings in my ears, "This is the Columbia Broadcasting System." (The United States was not yet in the war, so their transmissions were not jammed.) We even formed a group of friends who gathered in our apartment to study with a Viennese scholar and refugee named Dr. Shmuel Hubner (1891-1983).* An expert in Bible, Talmud and Hebrew grammar, he also had a doctorate. During the war years, Dr. Hubner gave me good advice which saved my life later on. He told me, "Whatever the Nazis tell you to do, do the opposite."

---

* I.C.: Dr. Hubner survived the war. In 1958, he translated (into Yiddish) and published (in Yiddish) two tractates of Talmud. He later settled in Brooklyn, and was a father and grandfather to rabbis.

SIX

Late 1941

BUT THOSE "GOOD" TIMES would soon disappear. The dark clouds were gathering above our heads and though we often did not want to see them, sometimes we had no choice. When we observed the Nazi soldiers from our balcony—probably on their way to France—they seemed invincible and we, fittingly, became discouraged. They impressed us as an unbeatable fighting force and we wondered how, and when, this power would be destroyed and could we be saved from the increasing dangers we were in? We wondered if we had a future left.

Deepening our sense of alienation, the Belgian media was taken over by the Nazis and became part of the German propaganda machine. Every day, the press reports celebrated new Nazi victories on all fronts, in the air and the seas. Headlines screamed that Allied aircraft had been destroyed and cities in Britain had been bombed and burned. Indeed, the news reports in 1941 were very depressing for us Jews.

In late 1941, legislation against [the] Jews of Belgium was in place and started to be enforced. The seventeen Verordnungen (decrees) issued by the Nazis included a "Jewish" curfew, which forbade walking in the street before 8:00a.m. and after 7:00p.m.; liquidation of Jewish businesses; enforced shipping of all merchandise to a certain ware-house; surrender of radios to an assigned place under threat of fine or imprisonment. Jews were not allowed in any movies, theaters or cafes. Jewish doctors and dentists could only treat Jewish patients. Other Nuremberg laws were in effect by the end of 1941 or the beginning of 1942.*

But, again, unlike the Jews in Poland or elsewhere in the East, we were not herded into ghettos where we might be subjected to depor-tation "raids," so we thought we were lucky. However, Jews in Belgium had to limit their places of residence to four major cities: Brussels, An-twerp, Charleroi and Liege.

Life went on. We circulated in the center of Brussels, which was full of black-booted German soldiers of all types—officers, Wehrmacht soldiers, SS troops, and *Feldgendarmes* with their steel helmets and peculiar, murderous gazes. It was disheartening that some Nazi edicts were carried out by Belgian sympathizers. The Nazis formed a kind of pseudo-government in Belgium called the *secrétaire général* for each ministry. For instance, General Gerard Romsée, a Flemish nationalist (who died in 1974 after being pardoned) was made *secrétaire général* of health and the interior and was very influential; and the *secrétaire général des affaires* économiques gave orders to liquidate Jewish busi-nesses.

Jews tended to obey commands out of [a] deep fear for their lives which led to a degree of degradation. We transformed from dignified human beings into unsure creatures who never knew what to expect. A puppet council of Jews (*Judenrat*), based on the *Association of Belgian Jews (AJB)*, was established on November 25, 1941, and its president

---

* Editors: The anti-Semitic and racist Nuremberg Laws of September 15, 1935 stated that only Germans of so-called Aryan descent were allowed to be citizens of Germany and placed limitations on the rights of German Jews. These laws were extended to Belgium in the wake of German occupation.

was the war-time chief rabbi, Solomon Ullman.* To what degree the *Judenrat* collaborated with the Nazis is a complex subject about which books have been written.†

But the establishment of the Judenrat, with all the criticism it spawned, oddly brought a measure of routine to Jewish life. Since Jews were officially banned from public, Catholic, and private non-Jewish schools, by the end of 1941, the Judenrat-AJB established Jewish schools and medical institutions.

Controversially, the organization also collected all the addresses of Jews in a kind of registry, threatening violators with severe punishment if they failed to register. Was this smart? Later, the Nazis used this registry to hunt down Jews. The majority of Jews in Brussels were spread out. It would have been very difficult and time-consuming for the Gestapo to find and arrest Jews for deportation, without knowing where to go. But by establishing the Judenrat, the detention and arrest of Jews *en masse* was made easy. Indeed, as I remember it, certain members of the Judenrat did assist the Nazis in carrying out their infernal plans. However, in retrospect, I am sure that the Judenrat was not aware of the Nazi's ultimate goal which included finishing them off too when they ran out of ordinary Jews to kill.

We chafed at the new anti-Jewish laws but life was continuing to be viable somehow, or so we thought. After all, the way we saw it,

---

* Editors: The Association of Belgian Jews, or *AJB*, was a council of prominent members of the Belgian Jewish community formed by German occupiers. Ostensibly, the organization's charge was to take care of the needs of the Jewish community; in fact, its main function was to register Jews for forced labor and deportation to extermination camps. Much like the *Judenrate* established by German officials in Jewish ghettos across Nazi-occupied Europe, the AJB was not trusted by the local Jewish community.

† I.C.: After the war, I recall that the surviving members of the AJB, including Ullman, were questioned but not arrested by the authorities. One Belgian Jew, whom I know well, and who managed to serve in the Belgian and British Armies, called him "Rabbi Nullman," a play on the name "Ullman," saying that the rabbi did nothing ("null") to assist Jewish servicemen in Europe.

there were no deportations (yet) and at least three main synagogues in Brussels were functioning: the big synagogue on Rue de la Régence; the Orthodox synagogue on Rue de la Clinique—[overseen by Rabbi Segolovitch]; and Rabbi Joseph Gelenter's synagogue on Rue de Lenglentier. There was also a smaller synagogue (Hasidic) led by Rabbi Krieger.*

But things were about to change suddenly. On Yom Kippur 1941, during the *Kol Nidrei* prayers at the Rue de la Clinique synagogue, when everyone was absorbed in the seriousness of the occasion, a young man burst into the *shul*, running and breathless. He screamed, "Jews run! The Gestapo is on their way here!" Not a human soul remained. For us, this was the end of praying in an organized service on Saturdays and holidays. We started to pray at home instead. Life was becoming increasingly unlivable even by our "tolerant" standards.†

[Editors' Note: This italicized selection has been moved from earlier in the memoir for clarity. The postcards mentioned in this section are currently in the possession of Israel's son, Ken Cappell.]

A word about the postcards from Poland: During the early years of the war (1939–1942), my father began some correspondence with friends and relatives marooned in the ghettos of Lodz and Warsaw. Drawing no distinction between his wife's family and his own, he wrote to every relative and close friend of whom he could think. His missives to Poland are lost but the postcards to him form a riveting body of work which sheds light

---

* Editors: The first two synagogues referred to here are the Great Synagogue of Brussels (now known as the Great Synagogue of Europe) and the Synagogue of Anderlecht, where Rabbi Segolovitch worked until 1940 and Rabbi Gelernter from 1940 until his death during the Holocaust. I.C.: Later, Krieger managed to escape to the United States.

† I.C.: It would be several years later, on Rosh Hashanah of 1944, after Brussels was liberated by American and British troops, that the large synagogue on Rue de la Régence would conduct prayers. Today it is the official synagogue of the European Union.

on Polish Jews; their family's relationships, concerns, and the tragedy that engulfed them.

Writing in Polish and/or Yiddish (the Nazis permitted Latin letters on unsealed cards) they initially, politely, asked for used clothes, money and news of other family members. Later, their tone became more frantic as they included pleas for food, or "esen" (in Yiddish), as one man writes in over-sized letters from the Warsaw Ghetto. There are "coded" messages used to describe imminent deaths, such as "regards" from long-gone relatives.

The senders in Poland were only partially correct in assuming that we were safe in Belgium from the Nazi peril and able to help them. They assumed wrongly (I think) that since we were not confined to ghettos, our lives were better. This was only marginally true. Amazingly, the mail system worked, more or less reliably, during those years and my father managed to write, send clothing and wire funds (he was not rich) from Brussels to Poland.

But by the summer of 1942, we, too, were in danger, and went into hiding in Brussels. By then correspondence stopped although I am not sure at whose initiative. Perhaps the majority of senders were deported to extermination camps such as Treblinka, Auschwitz and Chelmno (near Lodz).

My father stashed the postcards in stored furniture in Brussels where we lived, a wise move because we were arrested in April 1944. After the war, when it was evident the senders had perished, the postcards, still in the (now retrieved) furniture, traveled to the United States where they became (for my parents) a kind of paper tomb, the last "word" from their perished brothers, sisters, nieces, nephews and friends. I inherited the collection when my parents died in the '70s and '80s, and a couple of decades later I took them out of a gray filing cabinet in my basement and showed it to one of my daughters.

Loss of family was clearly not the only thing my parents endured. Gone was a sense of belonging that had defined their lives. After the Holocaust, all that was left were fossils of their original lives. The postcards, I imagine, were a comfort.

SEVEN

The Arrest of My Brother and the Enforcement of the Anti-Jewish Laws

THE ENFORCEMENT OF ANTI-JEWISH Nazi rules started to menace Jews already in the summer of 1941.* One day my brother, Charles, went to meet his then-fiancée, Sprinca ("Isa") Gliksman, in Antwerp in July (1941), just as anti-Jewish laws forbade Jews to be in the street after 7:00p.m.† Having missed the 7:00p.m. train to Brussels, my brother was on the "waiting" platform after 7:00p.m. Approached by Antwerp police and Belgian SS, he was given a summons to appear the

---

* Editors: During the first two years of the Nazi occupation of Belgium, before deportations began in 1942, Belgian Jews were subject to an increasing number of restrictive laws, including removal from the civil service, seizure of businesses and property, nighttime curfew, forced registration, identification with a yellow star, and the removal of children from schools.

† Editors: A bulletin published by the Jewish Telegraphic Agency on September 18, 1941 suggests that the curfew imposed on Brussels forbade Jews from leaving their homes between 8:00p.m. and 7:00a.m.

Israel's brother Charles (*left*) and Israel (*right*) circa 1946.

next day at the Antwerp *Kommandatura* [headquarters], at which he would pay a fine. He did not mention this event to us, and the next day went back to Antwerp to pay the fine in the *Kommandatura*.

Only, he did not return home and we did not know where he had disappeared. My parents were beside themselves with worry, as we all were. We found out later that, upon entering the *Kommandatura*, he had been arrested and sent to the city jail and then to Saint-Gilles, a neighborhood in Brussels. He was with other Jews (from Antwerp), including a Mr. Grajower, (whose brother was later my friend) for violating the curfew law. The fine was a trick and after that we learned not to trust the Nazis, advice buttressed by the warnings of the clever Viennese refugee, Dr. Shmuel Hubner.

Charles stayed in Saint-Gilles for three months and was then transferred for another 5 months to the far more brutal Nazi camp of Breedonk, which was housed in an old fort once in use by the Belgian military. In Breedonk, Charles met decent Belgian as well as Jewish people who were far from being criminals. But the Gestapo didn't care and soon turned Breedonk into a torture camp for arrested Resistance fighters and Jews.* Once we found out that he was there, my parents tried to enlist *"makhers"* [Yiddish: people with influence] to get him out. But it wasn't a simple matter. Charles stayed in Breedonk for six months and suffered from anti-Semitism, beatings, slave labor and hunger— all for violating the curfew for Jews by ten minutes.

In February of 1942, by some miracle, the Brussels Gestapo decided to release the group of Jews that had been arrested that day, including my brother. (The camp has been the subject of many books and articles.) His homecoming was an unforgettable event. Following a routine ring of the doorbell, there there he was, back at the home he had left eight months ago to go to Antwerp and pay a fine. We were all stunned, to say the least. He was properly fed before his release. The Gestapo hoped to make a positive impression on the Jews so when they [the Nazi occupiers] would distribute orders [for Jews] to present themselves for "work" in Germany, Jews would not resist or balk and go confidently (to their deaths) in Auschwitz. Unfortunately, it was a successful trick for many, and Belgian Jews by the thousands made the error of trusting the Nazis.

Charles told us that every day the prisoners in his camp were made to march to a tune called *"Breedonk! Ich kann dich nicht vergessen."* ("Breedonk! I will not forget you"), and for the many decades of life which followed (he survived the war and died in New York at age 89), he never did. Here are the full lyrics to the gruesome "song":†

---

* Editors: Breedonk was a detention camp opened by the Third Reich in a preexisting fort in August 1940. It held some 4,000 prisoners over the course of the war. Several hundred inmates died from torture, murder, or harsh conditions in Breedonk. Most of the prisoners were Jewish; however, members of the Belgian resistance and political resisters were also interned there. After 1942, Jewish prisoners were transferred from Breedonk to the Mechelen transit camp or to the Auschwitz-Birkenau camp complex.

† This song mimics another camp song, "Buchenwaldlied," preserved by the Boder Collection at the United States Holocaust Memorial Museum. For a full tran-

Und der Wald ist schwarz und der Himmel rot,
und wir tragen im Brotsack ein Stückchen Brot
und im Herzen, im Herzen die Sorgen.
O Breedonk, ich kann dich nicht vergessen,
weil du mein Schicksal bist.
Wer dich verließ, der kann es erst ermessen,
wie wundervoll die Freiheit ist!

And the forest is black and the sky red,
we carry a small piece of bread in our bags
and in our hearts, in our hearts our sorrows.
Oh, Breedonk, I cannot forget you,
because you are my fate.
Only one who has left you, can measure,
how wonderful freedom is!

We considered Charles's deliverance from Breedonk to be a miracle. And it was! After the release of some fifteen Jews, the gates of Breedonk were shut for good and rarely anyone came out alive. Six weeks later, Charles married his fiancée, Isa, in Antwerp. She had patiently waited for him while he had vanished, a foreshadowing of the tragedy that was to sunder their young, hopeful married lives.

I could not attend the wedding, for which my entire family traveled to Antwerp, because I caught scarlet fever and was quite ill with a high temperature. I lay in a dark room (because the light bothered me). The year was (February) 1942 and by Nazi law—a law that emanated from the *Feldkommandantur*—only Jewish doctors could treat Jewish patients and non-Jewish doctors ("Aryans") could not attend

---

scription and translation of the original: "Music and the Holocaust," https://holo caustmusic.ort.org/. According to his son Ken Cappell, Israel often sang this song during the last years of his life, as if to say: "I'm 99, and look at me, I'm still here."

[to] Jewish patients. However, there were very few Jewish doctors around and anyway we did not know any. However, the non-Jewish doctors we approached disregarded the Nazi edicts and treated me. Their names were Drs. Filet and Verhogen. And they visited me daily until I was cured.

EIGHT

The Noose Tightens

EVEN THOUGH WE MANAGED to navigate around the Nazis, we knew better than to let down our guard. We knew the Nazis were criminals and sadists. After all, as I mentioned, my father received heartbreaking mail from his terrorized friends and family in occupied Poland. We did not realize that we would be in the same boat a bit later.

But in the beginning of 1942, the noose was tightening around our necks. Compared to our relatives in Poland, we were okay, but not for long. True, we were still living in our apartment with the new Philips radio (with shortwave [transmission]) and listening to CBS directly from New York; we were sleeping in our own comfortable beds; using our own bathrooms and never short on food or clothing—even kosher food was available on the black market.*

---

* I.C.: Food on the "official" markets was rationed and of mediocre or poor quality. Business was still brisk. Selling was not the problem: rather, obtaining merchandise, which was in short supply, was. The currency was imposed by the Germans, who printed money whenever they needed to.

But the mood was somber because we kept hearing of German successes in the war. This was discouraging because we were praying for their quick defeat. It seemed like every day brought new victories for them on all fronts— Russian, African and Japanese [aka Pacific]— while the ring around us was getting tighter and tighter. We were fearing the appearance of new anti-Jewish laws. The entrance of the United States into the war offered a glimmer of hope, but our pessimism was very deep.

In his speeches, Hitler kept talking about the Jews, how they were responsible for the war and how they will pay for it. From these speeches I learned that the Nazis were liars. Hitler, himself, started the war and wanted it, while the Jews had nothing to do with it. In the beginning of 1942, as the "Final Solution" (headed by SS general —*Obergruppenführe*—Reinhard Heydrich) was being decided somewhere in Berlin; the plan was unbeknownst to us.*

I first saw Hitler's speeches (in stadiums decorated with swastika-bearing flags by the hundreds) on movie reels at movie theaters [and] later I heard them on the radio. He was spewing curses and threatening Jews with their annihilation. On the movie reels I also saw (for the first time in my life) huge slogans, blaring anti-Jewish sentiment such as "Der Juden sind unser Unglück" (The Jews are our Misfortune). This was very shocking. But I never thought the German people would actualize Hitler's mad fantasies.

After all, Hitler seemed clownish in my teenage eyes, with his silly, black mustache and his ridiculous imitation of the ancient Roman salutation. But so many adored Hitler and his theatrics! After the "Sieg Heil's" people would break into the *Horst Wessel-Lied* ("the Horst Wessel song" [otherwise known as *Die Fahne Hoch*, 'Raise the Flag']), the Nazi German anthem which had its own anti-Jewish refrains and

---

* Editors: The so-called "Final Solution to the Jewish Question," formulated at the Wannsee Conference in January 1942, outlined the Nazi plan to systematically annihilate European Jewry.

lyrics and was named after Horst Ludwig Wessel (1907–1930), a Nazi activist who was shot to death in 1930 for unknown reasons.

In 1942, we began to feel the impact of the anti-Jewish legislation. During the entire occupation period, the Nazis ordered all apartment windows to be blacked out by curtains, paper or any dark material in order not to show light inside. One evening, the doorbell rang unexpectedly. We lived on the third floor of a three family Brussels house located at 42 Rue de Lenglentier, not far from the Midi train station. When I opened the door, I was startled to see a Belgian policeman writing a ticket because we neglected to black out one of the windows adequately. It was punishable by a 20 mark fine and the cop handed the ticket to me.

The fine was payable in the German *Kommandantur* within three days. The fact that a Belgian cop delivered the Nazi ticket merely underscores to what extent the Belgian civil service was complicit in Nazi

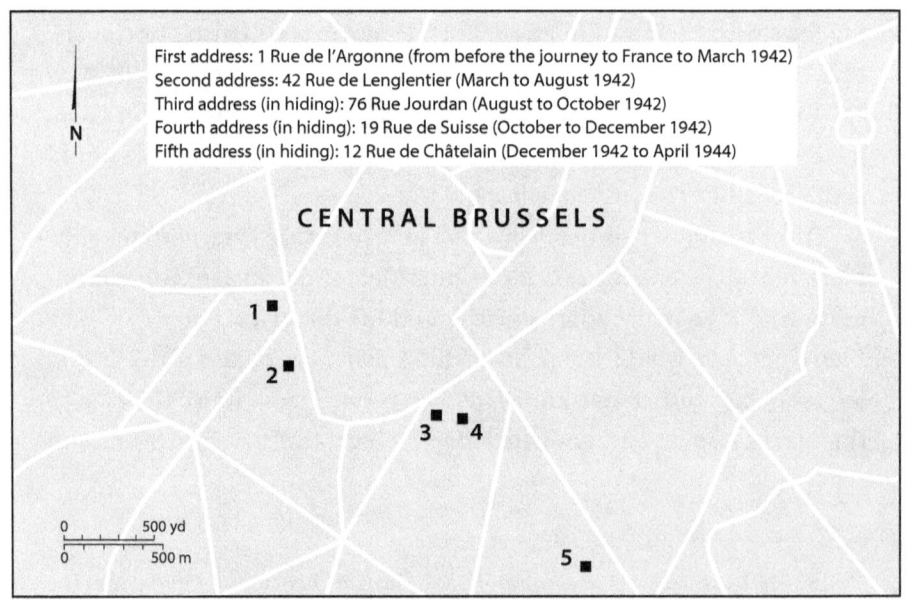

First address: 1 Rue de l'Argonne (from before the journey to France to March 1942)
Second address: 42 Rue de Lenglentier (March to August 1942)
Third address (in hiding): 76 Rue Jourdan (August to October 1942)
Fourth address (in hiding): 19 Rue de Suisse (October to December 1942)
Fifth address (in hiding): 12 Rue de Châtelain (December 1942 to April 1944)

N

CENTRAL BRUSSELS

1

2

3   4

0   500 yd
0   500 m

5

Israel's dwellings in Brussels during the war

regulations.* Remembering what happened to my brother in Antwerp when he wanted to pay a fine and landed up in Breedonk, I was reluctant to go to the Nazi *Kommandatura*. Instead, I went to the Belgian police precinct where the fine was issued and spoke to the *commissaire* (commander) of the precinct telling him that I was Jewish and that I was frightened to encounter Nazis, so I would rather pay the fine in the Belgian police station.

In a distinctly cold and bureaucratic tone, the *commissaire* explained that there was nothing he could do, and that the payment had to be made in the Nazi *Kommandatura*, on time, and by the person who received it. Again, his attitude reflected Belgian complicity in Nazi aims.

The next day I ventured out to the *Kommandatura* which was located on Rue de la Loi in a huge (former) Belgian government building which the Nazis had requisitioned. Helmeted German soldiers were standing guard on each floor. Trembling, I approached one guard and in my broken German, I asked him for the place to pay the fine. He pointed to the door of a certain office. With my heart practically jumping out of my chest, I presented the ticket and a 20 mark billfold to the Nazi clerk. He, in turn, stamped it and waved me on. I happily darted down the marble steps to the street—a free man. I felt lucky that this second encounter with Nazi authority was mild. But it was just the beginning, and it would not always be [so].

My brother and his pretty, Lodz-born wife, Sprinca ("Isa"), were happily married and rented an apartment on Avenue du Roi facing the beautiful *Parc de Forest*. Everything seemed to be so pleasant (for a change); the couple was happy and their apartment was spacious and

---

* Editors: In fact, Belgian leaders' complicity with the Third Reich varied city by city. The civil service in Brussels was relatively resistant to the Nazi persecution of Belgian Jews; for example, the mayors of Brussels's boroughs formally protested the introduction of the yellow star in June 1942. Civil service resistance also existed in Liege, while, by contrast, the authorities in Antwerp and Charleroi were largely complicit with Nazi instructions. Permanent exhibit, the Kazerne Dossin: Memorial, Museum and Documentation Centre, Mechelen.

Charles and first wife Isa circa 1941.

smart. They had elegant furnishings, and it was a mild spring outside. Charles was living the dream, punctuated only by the miserable presence of booted and steel-helmeted *Wehrmacht* troops and SS soldiers swarming in the street. Yes, our Jewish hearts were full of worries as if we could foretell that my brother's newlywed happiness was about to end horribly. Five months of married life, everything that he worked so hard to achieve, was about to melt away. This is what happened:

In July 1942, on the eve of the fast of *Tisha B'Av* (the ninth day of Av—a fast day) Isa, (as she was known) my new sister-in-law, took a train from Brussels to Antwerp via the town of Mechelen ("Malines" in French). Fifty kilometers and half an hour from Brussels, Mechelen was and is equidistant to Antwerp. She was going to Antwerp to prepare a pre-fast meal for her widowed father, Tuvia, and her two younger brothers, Maurice, 14, and Alex, 20. On that day, the Germans decided to start the Holocaust in earnest.

The State Security Police [Sicherheitspolizei], of which the Gestapo was a part, was stationed at the train stop in Mechelen. They boarded each train and asked for identity cards which by now were stamped with the bold red words *"Juif"* or *"Jood"* signifying a person's

Jewishness. All Jewish men, women and children were removed from the train. They were sent to an old military barracks in Mechelen which the Gestapo converted into a horrible "transit camp" and re-named SS-Sammellager the Kazerne Dossin. It was later referred to as the "ante-chamber to death" because it was from there that Jews were cruelly assembled and told (falsely) they were going to be slave la-borers in Germany, only to be sent to Auschwitz-Birkenau from which few (just 5 percent) returned alive.

Throughout the war, we never knew what had happened to Isa. She simply vanished. We hoped that she was alive somewhere in an eastern labor camp. After the war, we found out that Isa had become an early victim of Nazi persecution. She left Mechelen on the fifth transport to Auschwitz, on July 8, 1942, and vanished into the carriage car (closed cattle car wagons were introduced in Belgium later on in order to limit window escapes) heading for Poland, never even having had the chance to say goodbye. At twenty-one years old, her life was over. She died in the gas chambers of Auschwitz.

Of course, during the war, the existence of gas chambers was a secret about which we learned later from listening to the BBC. It took a long time for my brother to recuperate from the shock of losing the love of his life so abruptly. Charles was a broken man until the end of the war when he ascertained that she was dead, and he remarried. The Red Cross posted the names of survivors on the walls of a large build-ing rented from a Catholic youth organization.*

This is how the Yad Vashem website of Jews slain in the Shoah remembers the woman we called "Isa."

---

* I.C./N.G.: Charles remarried Pola (née Klein), also from Poland. Her father, Zusha, mother, and only brother, Yisrael, also perished. Pola survived with her two sisters, Gilberte-Jacqueline Kahn (or Kane) and Marie Dyner. Charles and Pola immigrated to the United States and raised four talented children, who, in turn, gave them many grandchildren and great-grandchildren. Despite the pain-ful losses both endured, they lived long and productive lives, and are buried near my late parents in the hills of Jerusalem, a city which Charles visited and loved.

"Sprinca Kapelusznik (née Gliksman) was born in Lodz in 1920. She was a housewife and married to Chaskiel (Charles). During the war she was in Belgium. Deported with transport V from MALINES, KAZERNE DOSSIN, Camp, BELGIUM to AUSCHWITZ BIR-KENAU Camp on 25/08/1942. Sprinca was murdered in the Shoah. This information is based on a Deportation list found in [the] list of the Jews deported from Belgium - Jewish Museum of Deportation and Resistance at Mechelen/Malines [Joods Museum van Deportatie en Verzet, Mechelen]."

NINE

The Holocaust in Belgium Begins

THE NAZI SECURITY ORGANIZATION, the Sicherheitspolizei-Sicherheitsdienst of which the Gestapo was part, established their headquarters on the beautiful Avenue Louise, built in the 19th century, in the *Residence Belvedere*, in building 453.*

"Final Solution" activities began with the arrival of subpoenas to the homes of all Jews in Belgium. In Brussels, delivery of the subpoenas was carried out by the Judenrat. In Antwerp and in other towns, it was delivered by the Belgian police, who were helpful to the German occupiers. In Antwerp, as mentioned, the Belgian police joined the Gestapo in raiding the Jewish quarters. Written in French and German, the subpoenas seemed innocuous at first—even ordinary. True intentions were well hidden. Trickery was a vital Nazi tool.

The subpoenas requested the Jewish recipients present themselves

---

* I.C: Eventually, they occupied numbers 347, 418, 453 and 510 after January 1943, when Brussels-born Jean Longchamp, a pilot in the Royal Air Force, mounted the solo attack on the headquarters at number 453.

at the barracks in Mechelen for "work" under the threat of incarceration in a German concentration camp plus confiscation of all possessions for failure to comply with the order. The sender was the military
commander of Belgium and Northern France and the military administration chief.*

My order, dated August 13, 1942 ("work order" no. 8319) had my personal information (name, date of birth, domicile and status) filled in
by hand. The document ordered me to report to Mechelen, at the Kazerne Dossin at Lierschesteenweg, (the name of the road) by Monday,
the 17th of August, at no later than 10:00a.m., to perform "work." Cyn-
ically, the subpoena added, "Your departure should be early enough in
order to guarantee your arrival on time."

As part of the elaborate hoax, and to lend it a "vacation" feel, I was
advised to bring the following items: food for fifteen days that was unlikely to spoil, such as canned vegetables, and certain grains; a pair of
heavy work shoes; two pair of socks; 2 shirts; 2 sets of linen to accommodate a bed; one bowl, cup and spoon; one sweater; my identity card;
my food rationing card and any other relevant documents.

I was informed that the rest of the instructions I would obtain
from the AJB, the Judenrat. The subpoena went on to say that I was
forbidden to "complain" to the authorities or to individual Germans or
Belgians but could register "complaints" once I was in the camp.

When my brother and I received the orders to report to the Kazerne Dossin, my father paid a visit to Chief Rabbi Ullman. He questioned Ullman about the purpose of the order to work and Ullman
said confidently that we would be sent to German fields. My father
went on to explicitly ask the rabbi why 8-year-old children had also received these orders to work, and Ullman replied airily that the children

---

* Editors: The two officers were Alexander von Falkenhausen, who commanded
  the Military Administration in Belgium and Northern France, and Eggert
  Reeder, his Chief of Administrative Staff. They were responsible for the political
  and economic administration of occupied Belgium, including the "Aryanization"
  of the Belgian economy and, later, the deportation of Belgian Jewry.

Israel Cappell's work order, Brussels, 1942, courtesy Ken Cappell

would "water the flowers." Of course, Ullman did not know the truth and was explaining away my father's concern's using his imaginative powers. The children had far grimmer destinies as we now know.

When my father returned from his visit to the rabbi, we had a "family conference" with my parents, brother, three married sisters and their husbands present. Once gathered, we made the crucial decision not to go to the Kazerne Dossin and thus to defy the German order and not to trust the Nazis at all. Of course, what this meant was that we had to go into hiding immediately because according to the order we had until the 17th of August 1942 to report to the Kazerne Dossin or risk incarceration in a German concentration camp.

We researched the neighborhoods where few Jews lived and knocked on doors where furnished apartments were for rent. We did not know this market at all and knew only that it was crucial to find people who would not inform on us and were in sympathy with our plight. Thus, we had to size up potential landlords according to the way that they "looked" at us. We had learned over the years to recognize anti-Semitic reactions to Jews, and we acted according to our instincts but in the end, we could never be sure about anyone and would have to assume a measure of risk. Finding a safe rental would prove to be a difficult task. We felt as if the Sword of Damocles was held over our heads from August 1942 to September 1944 (when we were liberated).

In the end, after many hours of searching, we found a suitable apartment, 76 Rue Jourdan, in a particularly un-Jewish part of town, in the Saint-Gilles, Brussels neighborhood. Mrs. Snyder, the landlady, was a middle-aged woman with an elderly husband and a skinny, 20-year-old son of medium height named Pierrot, a student at the Université libre de Bruxelles. They were Walloons, that is French-speaking Belgians, and their middle-class home was divided into furnished apartments. Mrs. Snyder was willing to rent the apartments to Jews to use as hiding places. She would also do all sorts of shopping for us, thus limiting our presence in the street and diminishing our chances of being caught. Of course, she would do all this for a substantial fee. But the conditions were acceptable to us, and a deal was sealed.

We quickly found a moving company to pick up all our furniture and belongings and deposit them in their warehouse till the end of the war period when we would pick them up, we hoped. The owner of the warehouse, Mr. Feguenne, also a Walloon, seemed a touch too happy to do the deal, as if he felt that one day he might inherit everything because Jews were vanishing. Either way, our apartment at 42 Rue de Lenglentier was completely emptied and we left without saying a

First Kapelusznik/Cappell hiding place,
76 Rue Jourdan, Brussels, courtesy Michaela Esposito,
Maia Gelerter, and Gillian Smith

word to the landlord or anybody else. We moved to the hiding place—
two bedrooms, a small kitchen and a living room—on Rue Jourdan
76. The apartment was adequately furnished. Our "group" at the time
consisted of my parents and brother, Charles. My three sisters (each
married) lived elsewhere.

The move was not easy. We moved separately so as not to attract
the attention of neighbors or passersby. As hiding places go, it was
rather advantageous for us because it was located in a part of the city

which had mostly rentals for transients, not families. But we still took precautions. We only took what was essential, such as a few items of clothing, books, prayer books and *tefillin* [phylacteries]. Though luxurious by the standards of the ghettos, we did not—for a moment— mistake our cheery abode for "normalcy." In the streets a war (against the Jews) was raging, and we were forbidden to go outside the house for fear of being denounced by Belgian Nazi sympathizers.

Without having the slightest information about our landlady, the blonde, skinny Mrs. Snyder had to be trusted with our lives on the basis of intuition. She claimed to have contacts in the underground Resistance movements and Pierrot said he was a member of the Resistance—points which inspired a measure of trust in these total strangers—but still it was decided that Mrs. Snyder's taciturn, elderly, gentlemanly husband would be relied on to do the food shopping.

I want to emphasize that Mrs. Snyder was not an idealist but rather a shrewd businesswoman in dire financial straits. The rental of this apartment to function as a hiding place was a business deal and everything had to be paid for. However, as time would tell, Mrs. Snyder was a decent person and not a traitor and did not exploit our situation.

Hiding was not an easy task. It was self-imposed imprisonment. The days became long, and the boredom was difficult to cope with. Jews were not allowed to own radios since mid-1941. But now that we were hiding, we felt we could break the German laws to some extent, and we listened to Mrs. Snyder's radio. The BBC and CBS (the United States was already in the war) were jammed by the Germans and we could barely make out the broadcast. However, we discovered that in Belgium the BBC Polish Hour was not jammed and Polish broadcasts were coming through loud and clear—and we knew Polish.

Much of the day spent [in] hiding was devoted to listening to news from the Free World and that became our lifeline. Hearing about a German defeat was a gift. However, until 1943 we frustratingly kept hearing of their victories.

Every day, the OKW (*Oberkommando der Wehrmacht*, aka high military command) announced daily news about military successes in

Russia; at sea (ships sunk by their U-boats); in Africa and, of course, they boasted about the devastating bombing of England. So the war news was plainly discouraging. It crossed our minds: Could it be that the Germans will win the war? Despite their successes, I felt the answer was "no," they will ultimately lose. But when and how long it might take, I had no idea. And how long could we possibly live in hiding, full of anxieties about going outdoors and being caught?

When we went into hiding, neither we, nor any other Jews, had the faintest idea that reporting to the camp in Mechelen meant a death sentence. I subsequently learned that 17,000 Jews reported voluntarily to the order issued by the Nazis, and they reported on time, bringing whatever the Germans asked them to bring. One of our friends, Mr. Hershel Bialogrod, [a man] in his fifties, who moved with his family from Poland to Antwerp and later, Brussels, had received the order to report to the Kazerne Dossin and came to us to ask our advice. We told him of our decision to "go clandestine."

His reaction was that we had made a terribly wrong decision. He said he was going to report for "work duty" in his best suit in order to make a good impression on the Germans and hoped to get a job as a clothing cutter, which he was.

I can only imagine his horrified shock when he arrived at the Kazerne Dossin and witnessed the screaming and the beatings of the SS upon presenting himself. The "reception" and the ill-treatment (this was even before the horrors of the trains) drove home the point that the Jews were trapped. It was too late for Bialogrod to turn back. He was already inside the cage, and he threw out a note from a moving deportation train asking whoever found it to forward it to his son, Moshe (who held a British Palestinian passport.)

Someone found the letter and forwarded it to his son, age 27, who, being a British citizen, was protected in theory. Moshe spread his father's urgent warnings to the remaining Jews not to report to the Kazerne Dossin because the "work" in Germany was a lie; it was, in fact, a likely death sentence. However, the fate of this son, Moshe, is not a happy one and shows how mercurial the Nazis could be.

In 1942, he was stopped in a Brussels street by Gestapo agents and asked for identification. He showed his British passport which they promptly tore up. Tossing him into their car, they took him first to their headquarters on Avenue Louise. From there, he was taken to the Kazerne Dossin in Mechelen and from there he was sent to Auschwitz, where he perished.*

When we heard about the letter which Hershel tossed out, we knew we had apparently made the right decision not to obey the order and not to report to the Kazerne Dossin in the first place. Our decision to go into hiding gave us hope and certainly protected us (for a time) from the nightmarish fates encountered by so many of those who, like our friend Hershel, did go.

At some stage Charles made a pivotal decision to register our family as Zionists to be exchanged for German nationals in Palestine. In every major European city before the war there had been a Palestine Office with a board of delegates from political left to right, tasked with, among other things, allotting the small amount of immigration visas to Palestine that the British authorized to give to the Jews in exchange for German nationals in Palestine. In Brussels, the Palestine Office was headed by someone named Yitzhak Shatan. A Dutch Jew, Benjamin Nykerk, was also involved.

The Belgian board was now meeting secretly to discuss how to divide the remaining exchange certificates among the still-living Zionist activists. My brother put us on the list to be exchanged, registering

---

* N.G.: The Yad Vashem database sheds light on the fate of the Bialogrod family: Hershel, 52, was deported to Auschwitz on the third transport from Mechelen, on August 15, 1942, with his son Noah, age 28, and Noah's pregnant wife, Roza (née Sendyk) from Berlin. Hershel, who also bore the name Asher, which he sometimes used as a first name, had a wife, Sarah or Sura (née Gibetz). She, too, was deported to Auschwitz in October 1942 on the 12th transport, as was their son, Moshe, age 27, who held the doomed British passport, and their daughter, Marjem Riterband, age 29, wife of Leibel. Born in Warsaw, the Bialogrods (including Marjem) dealt in manufacturing and selling underwear. A daughter, Chaya, survived and moved to Israel.

us for certificates as "Jakob Kapelusznik and family" and, separately, Charles Kapelusznik.

At the time, we had very little faith in the program and begged him not to go outdoors but he did not listen. Of course, he was right; the exchange program, negotiated with the Nazis and the International Red Cross in Geneva, would eventually play a huge role in saving our lives.

Charles also felt increasingly responsible toward the father and two brothers of his "disappeared wife." He invited them from Antwerp to share our hiding place on Rue Jourdan in Brussels because staying in Antwerp was no longer feasible for Jews without being arrested. They came and stayed with us even though we endangered ourselves by ex-

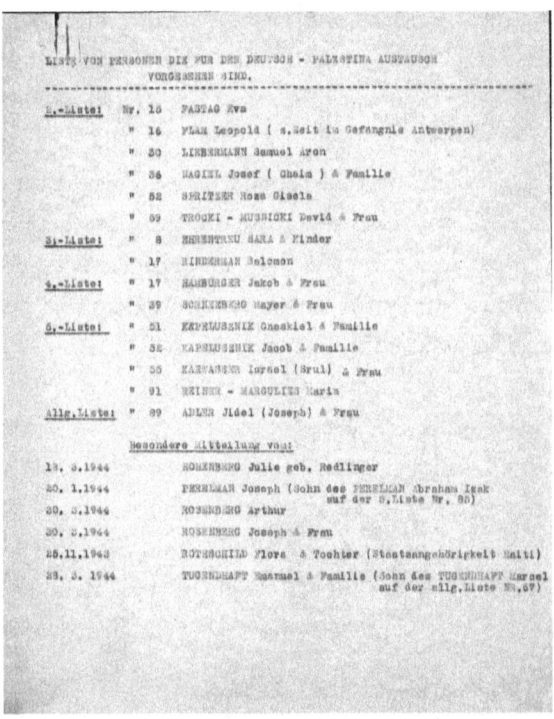

Kapelusznik family entry on the Palestine Exchange List, 1944, courtesy Kazerne Dossin, Memorial, museum and research centre on Holocaust and Human rights, Image 0010_A011713_000001

panding our group. Hiding large groups increased the chances of being exposed to the Gestapo.

Time in hiding passed slowly, as I mentioned. We kept busy by reading the depressing (to us) Nazi-controlled Belgian press which reported glowingly on various Nazi exploits. I began my day— like I had before the war— by reading *Le Soir*, which was once one of Belgium's most liberal, well-informed dailies. However, the new, Nazified *Le Soir* was a very different kettle of fish, acting as a mouthpiece for Joseph Goebbels' Nazi propaganda machine. Reading between the lines, we did find some evidence of Nazi defeats.

For instance, if the OKW (*Oberkommando der Wehrmacht*) reported that the High Command of the German military "made strategic retreats to better defensive lines," it meant a defeat or a large effort for light losses. But Hitler's continual, seemingly robust speeches in which he threatened to annihilate the *"Juden"* added to our despondency. We also read books, studied and socialized within our group, knowing that every day passed in safety was a blessing, and praying that soon things would improve for the Allied Forces and we might be free. But at the time it was only a dream. Frankly, I could not figure out what Hitler wanted from the Jews, as though we were some sort of major power. In most countries, we were not even one percent of the population and we lived with discrimination.

In mid-October, Mrs. Snyder told us that we could no longer safely stay at 76 Rue Jourdan and she proposed to move us to another house which she owned and rented in the same area, this time located at 19 Rue de Suisse. There was no alternative but to accept the offer and we all—including the hapless Gliksmans whose mother was deceased and whose sister vanished—moved to the new address. The apartment over there was larger and more comfortable than the previous one and boasted a backyard garden in which we could sit and breathe fresh air. One day, we noticed that to the right of us, another Jewish family seemed to be hiding. We later found out that, in fact, they were Dutch Jews. Many Dutch Jews seemed to be hiding in Belgium perhaps due to the numerous informers all around Holland.

The summer and autumn of 1942 were sunny and bright, but our mood was somber as German victories were piling up with no end in sight. We realized how great a burden it was to hide for a long period of time; to entrust one's life to total strangers who could call the Gestapo and end your freedom at any time as well as end your life! Also, we did not have the financial resources to pay for the hiding "operation" for more than two years, nor could we work.

But the Snyders did what they promised. They collected the amount of money agreed upon and did not try to extort more from us. Mr. Snyder continued to do the shopping and did not say much. His apparently much younger wife ran the business—renting out furnished apartments in various houses which the Snyders owned. As I mentioned, this was, strictly speaking, a financial venture. Mrs. Synder kept us as tenants as long as it was convenient for her. In the meantime, her son, Pierrot, introduced us to a friend by the name of Pierre Carnewal, who was also a student.

A brilliant young idealist, Resistance fighter and noble aristocrat, Pierre was a scion of a wealthy Belgian Catholic family. One of the kindest and nicest people anyone can expect to meet, Carnewal didn't have an anti-Semitic bone in his body. The son of a British father and a Belgian mother, he became an ardent anti-Nazi and was all too aware of Jewish difficulties under Nazi rule. His periodic visits were like breaths of fresh air.*

By the end of 1942, with the United States actively in the war, the

---

* I.C.: Carnewal was later caught performing a heroic act against the occupation and killed by the Germans. My great-nephew, Dr. Joshua Cappell, a grandson of Charles, sought to have him designated as a Righteous Among the Nations by Yad Vashem but I am unsure of what happened. Editors: According to documents from the Museum of the Belgian Resistance, Pierre Carnewal spent three years and one month in the resistance, from May 1, 1942 to May 7, 1945. Carnewal was arrested by the German police in September 1943 after a large-scale resistance operation, for which he was sent to a prison in Mons, Belgium and then deported to Germany. While he continued to be considered a member of the resistance after his deportation, Carnewal was thereafter presumed dead.

balance of power started slowly to shift toward the Allies' favor. But it was still a long way to go to the defeat of the Nazis and an end to the Jewish persecutions. A huge amount of mayhem and suffering would have to take place before the Nazis would capitulate. I kept a sizable map of Europe on the wall, with colored pins. I moved all the European fronts daily to keep up to date with the ever-changing situation. And the fronts were, indeed, moving! But anything short of a dramatic change in the war didn't mean much to our grim reality.

In December 1942, our landlady, Mrs. Snyder, came over to have a talk with us. Just by looking at her facial expressions, we knew that something [was] serious, bordering on terrible. And it was. Mrs. Snyder told us that the Jewish Dutch family hiding a few houses away had been arrested by the Gestapo and sent to the Kazerne Dossin in Mechelen for deportation to Auschwitz. Moreover, Mrs. Snyder said calmly that she had information that the Gestapo was planning to arrest us tonight. It was imperative to pick up and go to a different hiding place at once, adding that she had no other hiding place for us.

It was a Saturday and being Orthodox Jews, we decided to wait till sundown, not to desecrate the Sabbath. We quickly had to split up and find hiding places for all of us. Pierrot contacted Pierre Carnewal who arranged for the Gliksman clan to go to his home and stay there temporarily until a hiding place would be found for them. My sister Fanny had already found a place in Koekelberg, a Brussels suburb not far from my older sisters' hiding places.

We had no alternative but to send my parents to my older sisters' places; Charles and myself would go to Fanny. It was very risky for us to venture on a dark Saturday night in tramways to the other end of town. On the other hand, Saturday nights and Sundays were less risky than other times because the Gestapo agents were said to be in the red-light district having a good time. Thankfully, we all reached our destinations safely.

My sister Fanny and her husband, Josef, were hiding in a below-moderate hotel with about sixty rooms and few amenities. Upon arrival, we promptly went to sleep because we had had a very tense and exhausting day. In the morning when we looked around, we saw that almost the entire hotel was occupied by Dutch Jews who had been smuggled from Holland. Once in Belgium however, these people were strangers, ignorant of the different neighborhoods. Thus, they became very visible and easy prey for the Gestapo and/or informers.

We decided to leave the hotel as soon as possible. Because of the great concentration of Jews, the hotel might be a natural magnet for Jew hunters. In fact, it would be a miracle if the Nazis would overlook it somehow. Once again, we appealed to Mrs. Snyder and it was decided that, for a fee, her sister Mrs. Christine Carlier, also a petite dyed blonde in her fifties, would rent [us] a house in which she would live and we would hide. Like Mr. Snyder, Mrs. Carlier would provide for our shopping needs. We stayed in the hotel for two weeks, after which we found the "perfect house" at 12 Rue de Châtelain in the upscale Ixelles neighborhood of Brussels. Mrs. Snyder's sister moved in as did my parents, brother, sister Fanny, her husband, Josef and myself. It was around the end of December 1942.

In the meantime, the Gliksman family was relocated by Carnewal to an area occupied by many Resistance fighters, in the south of Belgium, amid the famous, wooded Ardennes mountain range. That area of Belgium, including Bastogne, a Walloon municipality near the border with Luxemburg, was very anti-Nazi and Jews generally found sympathy there and a willingness to help them.[*]

Our new house was narrow and two stories. There was a kitchen and two rooms in the basement which would be occupied by Christine, a kitchen, a small room and a dining room on the ground floor, a second floor, a small courtyard, and a toilet. It was decided that the ground floor would be divided between my parents and brother; the second floor would be occupied by Fanny, Josef and my other brother-

---

[*] I.C.: Thanks to Charles's initiative to invite the family to move from Antwerp to Brussels, the Gliksmans survived. In the Ardennes area, the Gliksmans were well-cared for by various underground agents and lived in good conditions.

Third Kapelusznik/Cappell hiding place, 12 rue de Châtelain,
courtesy Michaela Esposito, Maia Gelerter, and Gillian Smith

in-law, Maurice Dyner, who materialized after his landlady refused
to hide him; and I would use the attic, which had one large room. My
mother was designated to prepare the meals with Fanny.

I set up a kind of contraption in my attic room near the *mansard*
(slanted ceiling) window—where no one could see me—to make life
more livable. Using wood and a rope, I suspended a small platform
from the ceiling on which I would place a book, read or study. Next,
I would stand on a step which would face the book and poke my head
out of the window. In that way I could get some fresh air periodically
while reading. Planning and arranging all this was my main preoccupation during the hiding period of 1943-1944. I hung my map of Europe

and North Africa with the pins on a wall of my "situation room" in the attic. I kept busy, studying and reading and listening to the radio in the basement.

After a while, things settled down in the hiding place and life became routine. We could not use our ration cards which everyone needed to purchase food because use of the cards would immediately reveal our true identities to the Gestapo who would arrest us. Instead, we relied on false identity cards provided by the Underground. We were registered in a small municipality as Belgian gentiles and thus obtained food ration cards which Christine could use in food shops. Since there was no kosher meat to be had during the Nazi occupation period, we were forced to limit ourselves to fish, and since fish was not in abundant supply, we only ate herring—of which there was ample amount. My mother devised many different recipes: salty herring, pickled herring, fried herring, *gefilte* fish herring, and even herring "meat balls."

Bread and herring—in different forms—became our main food staple. Eggs, butter, hard cheese and many other foods were only available on the black market. Fruits and vegetables were rare and expensive. Again, we felt anxious about our money reserves running out, so we were reluctant to splurge on exotic foods.

It was now the winter of 1943. Days, weeks, and months were passing. Since we had no place to take a bath, and I naively believed the false rumors that the Gestapo was no longer quite so aggressive in detaining Jews, I ventured out to the Brussels public baths on Friday mornings. Equipped with tubs, showers, towels and soap, rooms were available for 30-minute periods, and sometimes bath houses had adjoining swimming pools. The problem was getting there. Though only 15 minutes away by trolley, the trip to the closest bath house was fraught with dangers—mainly at stops. I found this out the hard way.

For one thing, the Gestapo would board a car, accompanied by a Jewish man whom we called "Jack the *moser*" (Jack, the Informer, also known as "*Gros* Jack" or Fat Jack). Said to have been a doorman at a brothel in his old life, Jack specialized in recognizing so-called Jewish faces. If the "posse" consisting of Jack and the Gestapo saw someone suspected of being Jewish in the window of the trolley, they would push themselves into the car and force the unfortunate caught person to the cellar on Avenue Louise and from there to the Kazerne Dossin and to Auschwitz.

Things happened fast. That was the danger in going into the streets. One minute you could be heading for an innocent bath; the next minute you could be going to your death. In truth, I did not realize how treacherous the outdoors was at that stage. I had confidence, perhaps too much confidence, in my false identity card which claimed that my name was "Jules Moreau" and that I lived in a small town in southern Belgium in the Ardennes region.

The majority of Jews in Belgium lived in Antwerp and they were the most at risk for being arrested and deported. The local Antwerp police force happily joined the Gestapo in night raids on the Jewish quarter where they beat and mistreated Jewish men, women and children during removal from their beds and homes. These unfortunate people were taken in their pajamas to the Kazerne Dossin and then to Auschwitz. Cops in Brussels apparently refused to go along with these "arrests" and as soon as a German victory started to seem doubtful, the cooperation of other Belgian police forces (not Antwerp's) started to cool eventually.*

Back to the bath house. One day, the trolley that was taking me to the bath house was stopped. A bad sign. My heart was beating hard. A long line of trollies was forming as a result. Helmeted and armed military police started boarding the trollies and checking papers. They were not looking for Jews but rather for so-called saboteurs and young men who didn't respond to orders to perform labor in Germany. They could have arrested me as a Jew or as someone who failed to report for

---

* I.C.: Some Antwerp cops went on trial after the war for taking part in these brutal night raids but most were acquitted or sentenced and set free.

work in Germany. Other trollies were now piling up and the entire street was clogged with them. In response, a superior of the military police ordered the officers off because their actions were creating a big traffic jam. That was my lucky break. They did not get far enough in the trolley to inspect my identity card and I was safe for now. But I was shaking like a leaf. I learned the hard way that I was a Jew in hiding in Occupied Brussels. Not free, I stopped going to the baths [where I feared arrest].

Life in hiding continued to be difficult. We existed but made-believe that we did not exist. Our lives consisted of sleeping, reading, eating, praying, playing cards and chess, and listening in the basement to the BBC. "This is the British Broadcasting Company from London." That mere phrase, heard several times a day, was our lifeline and gave us hope that someday we would be free, normal people just like everyone else. Sometimes we could hear the Free French Radio from London, which always started with a song.

But in reality, the Germans still showed enormous power and the Allies' gains were too small to make much of a difference to us. How long will German soldiers fight fanatically under Hitler's instigation? We felt terribly discouraged and wondered about many things. *When will this end? How long can we hide and not be discovered? How long will our funds last? What will happen when our money runs out? Will we go hungry?* (Food was not abundant.)

In the Spring of 1943, there was a ring at the door of our hiding place. In came a Jewish woman with a five-year-old boy and their guide, a Flemish Belgian from Antwerp whose name was Franz. He claimed to be from an Underground group in Antwerp and was recommended by Tuvia Gliksman, my brother's one-time father-in-law, who was already hiding in the Ardennes region in southern Belgium. We did not have extra space for "guests" in our small house. But there was no alternative but to accept them. By coincidence, the woman was a sister of one of my customers in Antwerp, Mr. Zysman, who had a large store in Berchum-Antwerp.

Franz assured us that he would pay for any added expenses, and he kept to his word. We soon adapted ourselves to our new guests from Antwerp and we dubbed the small boy "Little Zorach." He quickly became the mascot of the house, and he brought some joy and amusement to the otherwise morbid atmosphere.

TEN

Pesach in Hiding

THE *EN MASSE* DECISION by Jews to show up at the Kazerne Dossin for "work" dissipated by early 1943 and now everyone fled into hiding. Indeed, the Jews were no longer naïve enough to report voluntarily to the Kazerne Dossin for "work in Germany" as had so many thousands before them: they knew that the place was a trap, and it was a fatal mistake to go there. Even so, no one really believed that the deportees— including the elderly and children—were being systematically gassed. After all, the Germans are a civilized nation [are they not]? How could they commit such atrocities?

Thus, the task of the Gestapo and their helpers became harder. They had to rely on a network of informers and arrest Jews individually. The difficulties that the Nazis had in catching Belgian Jews is reflected in the numbers. For the period of 1943 through September 1944, the Nazis detained and arrested fewer than half the number of Jews who came voluntarily in 1942. Nevertheless, the Nazis were still as brutal as ever. The "pick-ups" were accompanied by beatings and most Jews arrived at the Kazerne Dossin with marks on their faces and bodies suggesting that they had been beaten.

Ever since arriving [at] our house, "little Zorach" made life less monotonous. He did not understand what was happening and was quite clever and benefited our group with his mirth. Three months later, in 1943, Franz rang the bell again. This time he had with him Zorach's aunt (his mother's sister) plus her six-month-old baby. Again, there was no alternative but to invite the woman and her child in, even though space was super tight. Also, having a baby in the house exposed us to even more danger to be noticed by the Nazis. Still, we had to accept the young mother and her baby and be welcoming to our new "immigrants."

We now numbered eleven people—a dangerous, overcrowded situation. Our living arrangements were currently as follows: the two sisters from Antwerp, the baby, and little "Zorach" now occupied the basement; Mrs. Carlier had a room on the ground floor; we occupied the rest of the house. The short-wave radio remained in the basement. Sometimes we could hear Free French Radio, the [*Radio Londres* broadcast by the BBC] from London. It always started with a song. We lived in fear, terrified that we would not be around in the morning, even though by 1943 the Allied gains appeared to be more substantial and the German invincibility started to crack. It was possible to defeat these demons, but it was happening slowly. Germany was finally being defeated in the Soviet Union and in North Africa; and in American hands, the Germans, increasingly, were getting a taste of their own medicine. We cheered in silence and were somewhat more optimistic from the depths of our crowded hiding place. I kept moving my colored pins on my attic wall map.

But total victory by the Allies seemed illusory. Though the Allied forces were making steady gains, help was not forthcoming and freedom for Jews was far off. The Gestapo and the notorious informer, Jack the "Moser," were working relentlessly to catch people. We found out which of the people we knew had been caught. Pesach 1943 (Passover) was approaching.

How did we know it was Pesach? And how did we make Pesach in hiding? We found ourselves thinking about the coping methods of 16th century *conversos* in Spain during the period of the Inquisition.

They also had secret *seders!* But suddenly we had more urgent problems. Madame Snyder's sister, Madame Christine Carlier, became lonely and decided to take a lover. We discovered this quite by chance when one day we woke up and there was a new tenant in the house. Madame Carlier found a boyfriend, Mr. Paquet, a medium-size man with glasses and a heavy smoker. The sight of Mr. Paquet stirred up a feeling of uneasiness within us because we had no idea who he was. Nevertheless, his arrival was presented as a *fait accompli.*

Madame Carlier sensed our anxiety and tried to calm our suspicions about Paquet's honesty. Despite her assurances, we never grew to trust him. Jews were being hunted aggressively now, and we could not even take the risk of being in the street for a moment. We had become totally dependent on Madame Carlier; what she brought us to eat and so forth. She was not as clever or as reliable as her sister and failed to inspire us, but as with the decision to trust her sister, we had no alternative. She was, as they say, the only game in town.

We knew it was Pesach because in 1942 there was still a Jewish calendar being published in Antwerp and we had a copy of it. Second, despite the hiding conditions, we managed to be in touch with other Jews and were informed of "Jewish" news such as who was caught, and when the Jewish holidays were. Since our entire "group" was observant, keeping Pesach was very problematic. Packaged Pesach food, as we now know it, hardly existed in pre-war Europe (except *matzo*, of course) especially not during the Nazi Occupation. By some miracle, the Judenrat in Brussels was baking *matzos* and we managed to have enough for the *seders* and some for each day. Someone was sent to pick it up.

The arrival and departures of the various holidays gave us the feeling that time was passing—even though we were in hiding, and it was. First it was July 1942, summer, autumn, and winter . . . and then the entire year of 1943, with all the seasons and all the holidays. Our holiday meals were improvised. Though our seclusion was involuntary and we were dying to be free, we were happy not to be in the murderous hands of the Nazis.

In 1943, the BBC was reporting the mass murder of Jews, so we sensed something terrible was happening. We also heard about the Jewish leader who escaped from Poland and committed suicide in protest over the refusal of people to believe his eye-witness reports about the extermination of the Jews.* (British cabinet minister Anthony Eden was among those who refused to believe the reports, we later learned.) We believed the man (who ultimately committed suicide), but we also had certain reservations. Was it *possible* we asked ourselves again? Was the systematic slaughter of men, women and children conceivable in the 20th century? It was hard to believe. This question haunted us throughout the war years.

In the meantime, our schedule in the hiding place, in its second year, had a certain routine and monotony. We said our daily morning prayers, had breakfast with dark 'war' bread, black-market white bread, onions and radishes and ersatz coffee. (An egg was available once in a while and sometimes it was artificial.) Then there were 'cultural' activities, followed by a meager lunch with pickled herring, followed by more 'cultural' activities and dinner usually with fried herring. All this culinary activity kept my mother and sister Fanny busy! In retrospect, I give my mother a lot of credit for coming up with tasty dishes that could keep seven adults "happy." She was a kind of magician, and we could not understand how, without proper ingredients, she managed. But she did and her meals were like miracles. Concocting this food kept her busy all day long.

Our co-inmates, the two sisters and their children, managed their own household with supplies brought by Franz from Antwerp every

---

* Editors: The author might refer to Shmuel Zygielbojm, a Jewish official in the Polish government who escaped from Poland and later joined the Polish National Council in exile in London. On May 12, 1943, Zygielbojm took his own life in protest of the Allies' reluctance to intervene in the Holocaust after the Nazis' bloody suppression of the Warsaw Ghetto Uprising and their subsequent mass murder of Warsaw's remaining Jews. His courageous story was turned into a film, Śmierć Zygielbojma (*The Death of Zygielbojm*), released in 2021.

Sunday. Pierre Carnewal was our only visitor and sometimes he spent whole afternoons playing chess or card games such as *jeu de dames* [checkers] with us. He also discussed events on the various fronts with us as well as other topics. Pierre, a wonderful young man, had high moral standards, intelligence, a brilliant education and a great deal of idealism. He felt that it was his duty to fight the Nazis and assist the victims. He came to entertain us and often left his weapon with us to hide.

My brother, who was nine years older than me, could not get over the kidnapping of his newlywed wife on a train. He simply could not forget her and the life they once shared and he became clinically depressed. In the end, he found a legitimate job in an AJB-run old age home. By contrast to his black mood, I immersed myself in the study of the Hebrew Bible (*tanach*), which was the only Hebrew book we happened to have. I decided to memorize the Prophets. I found particular solace and hope in the study of the prophet Isaiah. His prophecy predicting the downfall of Nebuchadnezzar, king of Babylonia and conqueror of many kingdoms (including Israel), resonated particularly. I immediately likened Nebuchadnezzar to Hitler. Isaiah predicts his destruction by the king of Persia and proclaims, "How did you fall to the ground, you lightning star, you ruler of nations?"*

But at the same time, the Nazis were still "outside the walls" of the hiding places and picking up Jewish victims every day.

---

* Editors: "How are you fallen from the heavens, Bright One, Son of Dawn! You are cut down to earth, dominator of nations!" Translation by Robert Alter, *The Hebrew Bible*, Isa. 14:12.

ELEVEN

Fanny's Heroism

IT WAS NOW THE end of 1943. The German military suffered numerous defeats and had the ignominious fate [of] observing their soldiers being taken prisoner. But even as the Nazis suffered defeat after defeat, they did not relent in tracking down Jews. "Jack the Moser" was now working overtime to deliver Jews. Nevertheless, by the beginning of 1944, one could see the defeat of Nazi Germany on the horizon and my optimism was growing daily. It was a year of hope and the Nazi sympathizers among the Belgians started to see the Third Reich as (what the BBC called) a "sinking ship" and began to change sides.

Around that time Franz reappeared and told the two sisters from Antwerp who were hiding in the basement to pack quickly. He was smuggling them to Switzerland. Astonished and overjoyed, they packed up their belongings in a short time and went with him. Franz was an example of a Belgian non-Jew who was eager to help Jews. He took the women to the Swiss border and arranged a smuggler to meet them there. At that time, Switzerland accepted Jews with children who came to the border. Previously, this was not the case, and the Swiss would refuse the mass entry of Jews.

The sisters were, in fact, very lucky and Franz saved their lives.* We, on the other hand, were starting our third year in hiding. And we were worried about funds. Each month, we entrusted a man named "Monsieur Moreau" to sell off our grams of gold to provide money for our subsistence. Though the value of gold was rising, our reserve was disappearing, and we wondered . . . what will happen to us if the gold runs out and the war is still on?

Luckily, our hiding place started to empty out. First the Zysman sisters and their children left. Now, my brother-in-law, Maurice, decided to try to move back into [the home of] his wife and baby in the Molenbeek borough of Brussels. (Previously, the landlady had been afraid to keep him but now she relented.) All of a sudden it seemed quieter. We were excited to hear about German losses, but the Nazis were stubborn fighters and inflicted many losses as they went down, we understood. It quickly became the Spring of 1944 and I could stick my head out of the window in my attic "situation room" where the pins on the map were moving daily.

But despite all their losses, the Nazis intensified their hunt for Jews in Belgium—this was a constant theme—as if achieving the goals of the Final Solution were more important than defeating an army. With Pesach 1944 rapidly approaching, we were ambivalent about "celebrating" our second Passover in hiding. On the one hand, we would have a decent holiday thanks to the AJB/Judenrat's matzas and my mother's wizardry at whipping up meals. But we hardly felt free on this "holiday of freedom." We felt as though we were still slaves in Egypt enduring the worst kind of punishment. Our *seders* consisted of sitting and reading the traditional Haggadah, eating whatever my mother could put together and quietly singing the Haggadah songs so that no one in the area would hear us.

A few days later, on April 27, 1944 (the sisters, their kids, and Maurice [having] left just in time), there was a dreadful knock on the door

---

* I.C.: Franz came later to tell us that the sisters reached Switzerland.

in the middle of the night. It was the knock which we had been afraid of hearing since the beginning of hiding in July 1942. Shortly after the knocking—which was more like pounding—wild screams and the sound of the door being broken down filled the air. The killing machine devised by Hitler and his henchman had arrived, ready to swallow us. After breaking down the door, four Nazis ran wildly in the rooms and up the stairs, breaking chairs and beating anyone in their way.

I subsequently identified one of them as a Belgian Nazi called Journée (he had a crooked nose) and three others whom I later saw employed in the Kazerne Dossin—a huge Flemish trooper, another Belgian SS, and the leader, a German SS trooper, who was a sergeant. They had criminal faces and acted like wild animals in human forms, beating my mother, father and brother with the broken-off chair legs. (The Belgian SS were traitors who joined the Germans as soldiers and were typically low-class individuals, at the bottom of society, who enjoyed kicking and beating innocent people for no reason.)

Despite our precautions, we had anticipated this assault on our home and prepared a ladder in the attic, by the window next to the roof. Dressed in underwear, my sister Fanny, her husband, Josef, and I climbed out on the slanted tile roof in the pitch-black darkness of night. Emanating from below us were wild shrieks of the SS, mingled with the groans of the victims—namely our parents and brother. Who snitched on us and why? We had our suspicions. Within minutes a Belgian SS trooper appeared on the roof and bellowed that he saw us, and that he was about to shoot if we did not surrender and come down. While climbing, that SS man slipped and nearly fell off the roof.

Josef and I surrendered, and we came down the ladder, upon which the huge SS lunged at me, accusing me of attempting to push his soldier off the roof. He knocked me to the floor and stood on me with his boots beating me until I was bleeding from the nose and elsewhere. In the meantime, Fanny remained on the roof and managed to move further down "the street" until she reached the end of Rue de Châtelain. It proved to be a very fortuitous move which took guts and saved our lives.

Fanny Kapelusznik, undated

After the beating, I was taken down to the lower floor where I saw that my parents and brother were all bruised from the beatings by the SS. The beatings continued [and] when my father saw the SS attacking my mother with blows, he hollered, *"Oh mein Gott!"* (Oh my God) upon which the German sergeant exclaimed, "Your God is deaf and mute." At one point my father, in a naïve attempt to forestall our departure, acted ill and tried to convey the point that he couldn't walk and went to lay down on a nearby bed. One of the SS men took out his gun and said, "If you do not get up, I will shoot you." My father got up and received several blows for his efforts.

The four SS troopers escorted us to the waiting Gestapo car with its driver in front of 12 Rue de Châtelain. Our beaten and bleeding group departed for the short ride down Avenue Louise to the Gestapo headquarters. We were taken to a basement cell for men and women, which had a slanted floor tilted upwards. It was impossible to sit or stand on the floor and the men, women and children who shared our cell could only lay on it. There were several cells with that bizarre, house-of-horror feature in the basement.

In the meantime, Fanny eluded her captors and was safe. Later, she told us details of her escape although some of it I witnessed on the roof. She found an open skylight window at the end of the block of roofs, and she climbed in. Once inside, she found herself in a lone room, sat down and caught her breath. Worried about her family and unsure of what to do, daylight intervened, and she surprised the inhabitants of the apartment with her appearance seemingly out of nowhere. Standing in her nightgown, Fanny explained her predicament. Luckily, the people were kind and more than willing to help her.

The SS had found her identity card and posted guards on the street to look for a woman. Fanny intuited that; we ran off in such a huff. Who had time to take anything? So, her hosts gave her a man's hat and suit to wear to avoid detection on her way to Regine's hiding spot, which was out of the city and in a different neighborhood. She reached Regine and Maurice's hide-out safely.

The treatment we endured in the basement cell of the Gestapo HQ [headquarters] was my first bitter experience at the hands of the Nazis. Now it was perfectly understood why sane people, Jews, and others, fled and hid from them when possible. Every few hours the door to the cell would open and a few more unlucky victims caught in the streets or in their hiding places were pushed inside until 40 or 50 people had assembled, at which time we would be trucked to our next destination: the Kazerne Dossin. We stayed in the miserable basement cell for two days and two nights with very little food. We went to the toilets with permission and under guard. (You would think we were the world's biggest criminals!)

At one point a man's fat face appeared behind the cell bars. It was "Jack the Moser," the Jewish informer who worked for the Gestapo. It was the first time I laid eyes on this creature, and he resembled a pig in my eyes. He was a short, stout man, of whom it is said that his wife and children were deported. It is believed that he went to Germany with the fleeing Nazis after WWII and disappeared.

TWELVE

The Kazerne Dossin

A TRUCK CAME TO the entrance of the building at Avenue Louise, and we were pushed inside. It was filled to capacity with Jewish victims on the way to the dreadful Kazerne Dossin, an old fortress where they would wait until a sufficient number of Jews had gathered. Then, the whole lot would be sent to Auschwitz (usually 1,000 people). On the truck I made the acquaintance of a distinguished, middle-aged man who was very well dressed. His last name, he told me, was Shroubovitch. He was there with his wife, daughters and son. They were an aristocratic family, living (normally) amid great splendors.

Mr. Shroubovitch confidently told me on the truck that he was not worried because he had important connections and a lot of money and planned to be released upon arrival at the Kazerne Dossin. He even offered to send a message for me to whomever I wanted. Despite his strong belief of an imminent release, this wasn't meant to be. The Shroubovitch family stayed in the Kazerne Dossin until the 25th transport and then they were sent to Auschwitz-Birkenau.* The truck, with

---

* I.C.: I don't know if they returned from there.

its crowded cargo of worried Jews, made its way to the doorway of the Kazerne Dossin and entered the courtyard of the accursed barracks. It was a large courtyard surrounded by old, decrepit red brick buildings with entrances on all four sides. Some buildings were painted yellow. The courtyard was empty. Jews were rushed out of the trucks by Flemish SS men. Occasionally these SS would slap or kick the traumatized, hurrying Jews off the truck while shouting *"shnell, shnell"* (faster, faster). Their voices still ring in my ears.

Whenever a transport of Jews arrived from the Gestapo holding cell, no one was allowed in the courtyard except the Jewish *"pakn treger"* ("package carriers") or "porters" whose job it was to carry off the luggage of the new arrivals so it could be looted. Once, some Jews were caught carrying their own merchandise to the barracks, thinking they might have some use for it. They were punished and everything

Courtyard, Kazerne Dossin, 1942, courtesy Kazerne Dossin, Memorial, museum and research centre on Holocaust and Human rights, Image P000749

was confiscated by the "porters." Seeing all this, I quickly realized what sort of deep trouble we were in. We were in hell and escape seemed impossible.

On the left side of the courtyard were young Jewish women prisoners who sat at long wooden tables, taking from the new arrivals their small possessions, photographs, valuables, watches, money, house keys, home addresses, and identity cards. This was called the *Aufnahme* or "reception" desk. The arrested Jews were now possession-less victims, reduced to destitute human beings, dependent on the cement bread and watery soup which the SS provided.

So-called "assembly camps," like in Mechelen, Westerbork and Drancy were geared to begin the dehumanization process of the Jews.* The Kazerne Dossin was the beginning of the end. All that the Jews possessed was confiscated and prisoners were reduced to fighting among themselves for every crust of bread or potato skin. In retrospect, the Jews were being made ready for extermination.

We passed through the *Aufnahme* and at the end, we were allowed to enter the courtyard where the prisoners were mingling with the newly arrived. Assigned to Hall no. 13, we encountered about 100 people there: children, adolescents, adults (men and women), the elderly—a real potpourri. I kept thinking that these people once had bedrooms, dining rooms, salons and kitchens. Now they were crammed together on lice-infested, straw mattresses. Even so we all thought—me included—we would survive this hell. But most did not survive, and the hell merely got worse.

The Nazi "players" in my day were:

Johannes (Hans) Frank, a former policeman who had the rank of deputy major. Frank accused the first commander, Philip Schmitt, of embezzlement (from the Reich) and Schmitt was re-assigned. Schmitt

---

* I.C.: According to the Kazerne Dossin: Memorial, Museum and Documentation Centre, one man actually died of mistreatment in the Kazerne Dossin in Mechelen and some 50 others died there of other causes.

"proved" his insane sadistic streak first as the commander of Breedonk. Among his vicious activities I learned: setting his German Shepherd, Lumpy, on inmates, an attack which once caused a twenty-year-old Jewish man to have his leg amputated.

Frank's associate, the notorious anti-Semite, Max Boden, (same rank as Frank) who, too, started his career as a policeman (in Leipzig) and became a registered member of the Nazi party in 1928, [and] an SS officer known as "Moshe Genauer" (Moshe the Precise). The latter's specialty was to punish elderly Jews by making them stand against a wall for a prolonged time because they failed to salute him properly (he thought). Other than this "pleasure" he had little interaction with Jews.

Of the Flemish (Belgian) SS who stand out was the vicious Ludwig Van Kol, the man we called "Ferde Kop" (or Horse Head) because he

Ferde Kop,
courtesy Ken Cappell

was tall, strong, stupid, uneducated, and his head and face resembled that of a horse. But he was great at his job: beating and terrorizing Jews. Next, there was a skinny Flemish SS trooper whom we called "Moshe Patcher" (Moshe the Slapper), because he used to slap people when they least expected it, such as if they marched incorrectly or asked him a question when he didn't quite feel like answering. A Flemish SS known by the Jews as "Moshe Pisher" (Moshe the Urinator) got that nickname because he had a sour face as if someone just urinated on it, but he was harmless and had a minor role in the camp hierarchy.

I recall a certain Flemish SS whose name was Albert. His job was to bring the mail from the camp's office to the Gestapo headquarters on Avenue Louise. Finally, there was a man named "Journée" (it means "day" in French), a big, scary-looking man with large teeth who resem-

Dagobert Meyer, courtesy ENG: National Archives
of Belgium (NAB) [Brussels], Aliens' Files

bled the fictional monster in *Frankenstein*, the novel by Mary Shelly. Journée was the most violent SS officer in the camp. There were others but we barely knew them—although we were aware of their presence— such as the Belgian SS guarding the main buildings and roof, watching for escapees.

The Jewish prisoners also had leadership and personnel. First, there was the Austrian opera singer, Dagobert Meyer, who was probably half Jewish. Some memoirists recall him in a negative light but he played a significant role in saving my life. A tall, handsome singer of important operatic parts in Vienna, Meyer was *Lagerführer* (camp leader) and served as the conduit between Frank and the Jewish prisoners. He led the morning exercises in the courtyard, the marches, and the distribution of work assignments and had two assistants, Mr. Voss, a tall, handsome, blond, German Jew (who looked more "Aryan" than either Hitler or Goebbels) and Mr. Krauss, another German Jew; both of these men played minor roles.

Lisa Lotte was Frank's secretary; Eva Fastag, who was very Jewish-looking and whose extended family I knew, was Boden's secretary; my "hall leader" was Mr. Gingold, a diamond dealer from Antwerp; and my parents' *steuben elster* [room leader] was Mr. Sandzer. (Handsome, kind, aristocratic and athletic, Sandzer escaped the Warsaw Ghetto and reached Belgium. There, we learned, a Belgian baroness, who was romantically involved with an influential German general, simultaneously met and fell in love with Sandzer. She intervened for Sandzer with the general after Sandzer was apprehended by the Gestapo. Frank gave the Jewish man a job and treated him especially well. Sandzer, believed to have a daughter in Poland, was well-liked by all, and befriended my parents.)

Filling out the Jewish leadership were two doctors and two nurses who ran the infirmary known to the Germans as the *lazarett*. Dr. Singer, a refugee from Vienna, came from the torture camp of Breedonk, where he was my brother's friend during Charles' incarceration, and Dr. Parnass, whom I believe was a German Jewish refugee.

Both doctors were fine gentlemen who did what they could with their meager supplies to alleviate the misery of the unfortunate sick and injured inmates.*

There were also some notable personalities in the camp such as Felix Nussbaum, the German-Jewish artist who was a prisoner when I was, and was deported, and Colonel Tolkowski, a retired colonel in the Belgian army who lived in Antwerp with his prominent family. Tolkowski was not deported until the last convoy because of the apparent intervention of Queen Elisabeth of Belgium with the Gestapo authorities.†

At some stage, I was called from the courtyard into Frank's office which was located in the front section of the main building. My brother Charles optimistically said I was probably going to be released by error (instead of him, he thought, who had legally worked in a Nazi-approved old age home.) The reality was very different. Surrounded by Frank, Boden, and Journée, Frank read a letter from the Gestapo headquarters in Brussels accusing me of attempting to throw an SS officer off the roof when he was in pursuit. I denied it but to no avail. A rain of blows, from front and back, came down on me and blood flowed from my nose and other parts of my body. Boden and Journée, the Flemish SS, were particularly brutal.

Frank ordered Journée to take me to what they called "the bunker." A four-foot square hole in the ground, covered with a heavy metal cap such as one might see on the sidewalk under which there are electrical cables. There were several of these "bunkers" for "very dangerous" prisoners. Every day, a meager ration of bread and water was lowered into these structures. The prisoners stayed there until the next trans-

---

* I.C.: Singer survived the war and moved back to Vienna. Parnass also survived and married a fellow prisoner named Jenny after the war. They lived in Queens, New York.

† Editors: Elisabeth of Bavaria, the German-born Queen of Belgium, leveraged her status to resist the Nazi assault against Belgian Jewry.

port when they were removed (already half-dead from the brutal in-carceration) and were loaded onto the last cattle wagon. They traveled with the *"flitzers"* (escapees) to Auschwitz and once there, I was told, they were executed (by shooting) immediately at the so-called "wall of death" and were not considered for labor and did not undergo any "selection."

On the way to the bunker, I tried to tell Journée that I did not do what I was accused of, only to get another beating (on my head) from the Flemish SS officer's heavy hand. A small ray of hope emerged when I heard Dagobert Meyer say to a nearby Frank, "I do not think this boy is capable of doing what he is accused of." Why he said this, I have no idea, but by some miracle Frank listened to this remark and ordered Journée to take me instead to the *flitzersaal* (room of escapees) rather than to the bunker. Journée escorted me there and it was Room no. 1. I was given the special insignia of a *flitzer*—a red armband to be worn at all times and my head was shaved. This was how *flitzers* were immediately identified to the SS (and anyone for that matter.)

Each room or *saal* was designed to accommodate one hundred prisoners. The sleeping arrangements consisted of wooden bunks with three sections (one on top of other). Each section had a mattress filled with straw and lice. Thus each prisoner kept his belongings, slept, read or relaxed in a kind of cage. All these structures, I am sure, were designed by Nazi psychologists to dehumanize the Jews prior to extermination. The only advantage to being in the *flitzersaal* was that there were only seventeen of us at that time in our *saal* (hall) and no children and less noise. This made sleeping easier while the regular halls held at least one hundred inmates and whole families.

We were 16 men and 1 woman—the non-Jewish Mrs. Peters, a communist. I never knew exactly why she was sent to the Kazerne Dossin, and not being naturally talkative, she preferred not to shed light on the matter. She was later transferred to another jail.

After sleeping for two nights on the slanted wooden floor in the cellar of Gestapo headquarters on Avenue Louise and following a very painful (literally) and traumatic day, I slept through the night on the straw, and woke early next morning only to remember what sort of hell I was in—no wonder they called the Kazerne Dossin the "antechamber to death." Instead of the bunker punishment which I thankfully managed to avoid, I was ordered to do the *am dreckigsten* work (the filthiest work) in the camp.

This filthy work consisted of collecting a large, barrel-type drum or setup in the middle of each room, serving as a toilet to the one hundred inmates. By morning the drum was full of urine and excrement. My job was to remove all the drums (in the entire camp) on a hand truck to an area where they were disposed of. One day, Dagobert Meyer whispered to me secretly that: "Soon I will reassign you away from that filthy job and give you a 'clean' one." Till then I had never seen or heard of him. But later I did learn of Meyer's renown as an opera singer. Fact is, to this day, I have no idea why he decided to save my life, without knowing me or expecting anything in return. He watched over and guided me down a very dangerous path until my liberation.

The first morning in camp was the start of my "job." Room after room, I wheeled out the smelly refuse, performing my duties methodically and calmly, knowing that it was a temporary assignment. Luckily, I was not hindered or beaten by the SS soldiers on duty. After this "charming" job, I joined the camp routine, and washed my face and body parts in the washroom where dozens of people would clean up at the same time.

The washroom was a simple, stone place where cold running water emerged from multiple faucets. After washing, there was a lineup in the courtyard for physical exercises (gymnastics) and then a forced march around the courtyard, in step, according to the whistling of "Jackie the Whistler"—a Dutch Jew who normally performed on Dutch radio.* The march was where the SS had the opportunity to beat those who were not in step, typically elderly men and women who could not keep

---

* I.C.: Sadly, Jackie was deported on the last transport when the Nazis were desperate to send any Jew they could to Auschwitz.

the brisk pace. After the exercises and the marching, Meyer would issue a whistle (of his own), and this would signify that we were free to stay in the courtyard and socialize.

I met a kindly middle-aged fellow *flitzer*—only a real one—named Sholom Silbershatz from Brussels. He had escaped from the infamous twentieth transport which was stopped and attacked by three lightly armed young men, Youra Livschitz, a young Jewish doctor, and his two non-Jewish Belgian friends, Robert Maistriau and Jean Franklemon— members of the Resistance. The train was on the Mechelen-Leuven track and stopped between the municipalities of Boortmeerbeck and Haacht. Guarded by one officer and fifteen men from the Sicherheitspolizei, (Shupos) who came from Germany, there was a shoot-out.

Sholom Silbershatz, aka Szmul Szulem, undated, from the "Give Them A Face" Portrait Collection, courtesy Kazerne Dossin, Memorial, museum and research centre on Holocaust and Human rights, Image KD-00017-XXVI-0058-ZYLBERSZAC

Maistriau was able to open one wagon and liberate 17 people; others escaped without any connection to the attack. In all, 231 people escaped: 90 Jews were recaptured and put on another transport convoy; 26 others were killed; and 115 succeeded in escaping, according to reports which I have read.*

Silbershatz was one of the escapees and enjoyed a year of freedom until he was caught a second time and brought back to the Kazerne Dossin. He was in the *flitzersaal* with me and other escapees. Silbershatz was my neighbor on the next straw mattress and despite our age difference (he was much older and had a son my age), we became best friends, and encouraged one another at different stages. His wife and son were in hall no. 13 (on the left side of the *flitzersaal*). An optimist by nature, Silbershatz would tell me "Don't worry, we will outlive them" when he saw that I had a morose expression on my face. Sadly, he did not live to see his prophecy come true.

The weather was nice and warm, and my wounds (inflicted by the Nazis) were beginning to heal quickly. My hair also started to grow back, and Meyer took his role as my protector seriously. He advised me to hide when the barber, a nasty German Jew surnamed Goldberg came. Meyer pointed out that the bald head identified me as a *flitzer* and could attract the unwanted attention of the SS on duty in the courtyard whose sole job was to pick on Jews (among the prisoners) who didn't conform to their precise instructions and to torment them.

Punishments included beatings and standing at the wall for hours with one's hands up. Influential SS men such as "Ferde Kop" (Horse Head, aka Van Kol) and "Moshe Patcher" excelled at these torments. When we had to line up, Van Kol would enjoy stepping on someone's

---

* Editors: Israel may be slightly off in his accounting. The BBC reports: "Of the 233 people who attempted to escape from the 20th convoy with Simon Gronowski, 26 were shot that night, 89 were recaptured and 118 got away." "Escaping the Train to Auschwitz," *BBC News*, April 20, 2013, https://www.bbc.com/news/magazine-22188075

foot. Showing any sign of pain—like a grimace or a cry—would provoke an additional slap in the face. He, too, particularly enjoyed torturing the elderly. Nevertheless, socializing in the courtyard in small circles was still the main activity of the day. People made acquaintances, found out what was happening on the various fronts, how much closer we were to our liberation from this hellish place.

Across the narrow street from the entrance of the Kazerne Dossin there were other barracks occupied by the Wehrmacht. The recruits were mostly older men from what I could tell. Since the war was going badly for the Germans, these Wehrmacht soldiers were more sympathetic to us and our plight. But since contact such as conversing was strictly forbidden, we had no opportunity to speak to these men except when they came to shower in our washroom when their own was overcrowded. However, a roly-poly man known as Mr. Tuchmayer, in his sixties, succeeded where we all failed. Tuchmayer was an active Zionist, and part of the General Zionists. I believe he was on the Palestine Exchange List.

One of the most interesting personalities in the camp, Tuchmayer, arrived in the camp toward the end of its existence, and managed to have information about all the battles. He elicited this from the Wehrmacht soldiers, when they were waiting to use the showers. As the news for the Germans became worse and their defeats in Italy, Russia, and Africa became well-known, the Wehrmacht soldiers saw their end approaching and shared their anxieties with Tuchmayer. If Tuchmayer had news, a circle would form around him and the good news (that the Germans were losing the war) would spread in the camp. At this, Boden would also come down to the courtyard and say (in German), "Tuchmayer, you have news? I would like to hear too." Of course, at the sight of Boden, the circle of Jews would rapidly disappear.

It is the nature of humans to adapt to hard conditions, and so, too, I became accustomed to "life" (if you can call it that) at the Kazerne Dossin. I will now elaborate a bit on the food we ate there: I should start off by saying that upon arrival at the camp, we were issued a metal Bordeaux-colored soup plate and an ersatz (substitute) metal spoon and fork; knives were not allowed. One had to stand in line to get the soup into the soup plate. This was "served" with a piece of ersatz bread which tasted like cement. In the soup, sometimes one could find objects such as watches or razor blades floating around. This happened because certain packages were opened by the SS soldiers, who stole various items. The food went straight into the soup and the [concealed] blades emerged. (Normally razor blades, considered a weapon, were forbidden to the prisoners, except to the barber. Nevertheless, they were smuggled in food by some families sending packages and then inadvertently tossed in the soup.)

One could not survive without food packages from the outside, which the Nazis somehow allowed. The distribution of the packages was a very important event. Twice a week, a truck from the AJB would deliver the packages and pick up the empty bottles, boxes, towels and string that belonged to the organization. All the packages were gathered in a single place in the courtyard and Kessler, one of the Jewish kapos, who was also a kapo of my brother's in Breedonk, called out the names on the packages.

Since my family consisted of five persons—parents, brother, brother-in-law Josef, and me—our name was called five times for the five food packages, and five times for each bottle of apple cider—items sent by my escaped sister, Fanny. The frequent calling of our name by Kessler (ten times) caused one prisoner named Hamburger, to include a rhyming line about my father in a [mixed] German/Yiddish poem: *"Der Herr Kapelusznik mit zayn frum gebet is der Konig die Pakete."* [Mr. Kapeluznik with his pious prayers is the king of the packages.]

Every day at 4:00 p.m., the window of the kitchen opened for distribution of hot water. Mostly the elderly lined up in front of the window, some with thermos bottles in hand. While waiting their turn, SS Van Kol, (the "Ferde Kop") would amuse himself by stepping on someone's foot or grabbing a thermos from an older person's hand and breaking it on the floor while laughing. He would jeeringly say in German, "Write to the AJB and they will send you another one." Needless to say . . . losing a thermos was a catastrophe because it meant that the unfortunate prisoner no longer had a receptacle in which to put hot water. Thus, he or she was deprived of a warm drink—a necessity.

Later in the afternoon "soup" was distributed from the kitchen supplied by the Belgian Winter Help Organization. The soup consisted of water and pieces of cauliflower swimming in the middle. But with all this heartache, we somehow knew that life in the Kazerne Dossin was a "luxury hotel" compared to say Auschwitz, a living hell which, we later learned, hungrily consumed lives every single day.

Harassed all day in the courtyard by Boden, Horse Head and "Moshe Patcher," it was soon time to return to the straw and lice and to try to sleep. But the Nazis still had energy to amuse themselves by torturing us. Usually one of the SS officers, sometimes Frank with his German Shepherd dog, would arrive at night for inspection. If it was Frank and his dog, he would let the animal jump on the prisoners, terrorize them, smile and leave.

In the meantime, Frank lived like a king. He ate well and maintained a private pig stall, [for] which a Dutch Jew served as caretaker—a job which saved the man's life. Frank also had a convertible Mercedes (probably stolen) with a chauffeur, a Jewish prisoner, who was a diamond dealer from Antwerp in his normal life. His last name was "Fingerman" and he, too, survived the war.

Sometimes, the Nazis amused themselves by acting out a "comedy" about healing a sick Jew in camp only to gas him upon arrival in Auschwitz. They undoubtedly did this to heighten our already-acute anxiety, but it was a rare breach of secrecy and suggests that the rank and file may have suspected to what fate the Jews were heading. This contradicts Frank's later testimony (at his post-war trial) that he had no idea that he was sending Jews to die by gas, and had he known the truth, he, too, would have gone to Auschwitz. Hard to believe Frank's claims.

But the main "action" of the day was when a truck holding a future convoy of victims arrived from Gestapo headquarters in Brussels, an unfortunate spectacle that could happen as often as twice a week. When this happened, all veteran inmates were ordered into their rooms. The Nazis called out, "Alle in ihrem Zimmer" ('All to their rooms') to make way for the newcomers. After this command, a truck entered the camp, and out came men, women and children—all bewildered, scared and tired, taken (in many cases) from their warm beds and brought to this miserable, yellow-walled place.

Their degraded state was no surprise. All had been kept for days in the basement of Gestapo headquarters with the slanted wooden floor in a small cell with no window until being placed on a convoy from the Kazerne Dossin at Mechelen to Auschwitz.

Typically, Frank and Boden watched as the future deportees jumped out of the truck. The SS would add to the prisoners' profound disorientation and fear by screaming and beating victims. (Truck transports to the Kazerne Dossin in Mechelen usually consisted of 25 to 30 people.) It was a horrific sight. Sometimes I pondered about the color "yellow" and its use by the Nazis. The inner walls of the Kazerne Dossin fortress were yellow, as was the mandatory Star of David patch that Belgian Jews had to wear as of 1942.

The frightened group of newly arrived Jews was assembled in the courtyard, as in previous times, and marched before the *Aufnahme* just as I had been. Anyone attempting to hide a valuable object (such as a diamond, and there were many diamond dealers caught) would be beaten because from that moment on whatever property the prisoners had was considered to belong to the Reich, and hidden valuables were regarded as property looted from the German Treasury.

(In an earlier period of incarceration in the KD, my wife, Eva, who worked at the *Aufnahme*, did agree to hide a packet of loose diamonds for a man who requested it, named Friedman. She motioned him to bury it on her desk amid her papers and returned the packet to him in the courtyard. Had she been caught, she would have been punished and doubtlessly sent on the next convoy to Auschwitz. Though I commend her for her valor, I don't think the diamonds saved Friedman, although sometimes jewelry bribes did help save lives.)

After the new arrivals were registered and their valuables stolen, they could go into the courtyard and mix with other prisoners. Circles formed around them to see who they were (if they were an inmate's relative or acquaintance), and what news, if any, they brought of Brussels (if they were from there) or of the world. The arrivals were given rectangular, green pieces of cardboard with black number transport numbers written on them. In this case, they were assigned to transport no. 25.

All Jews arriving at this time were caught while hiding because no one was coming to the Kazerne Dossin voluntarily at this stage. The news we received from the new arrivals was always similar. The Nazi newspapers such as the *Brüssler Zeitung* and the other Belgian newspapers newly run by Nazis kept repeating new victories amid "strategic" retreats. From this we deduced that by May 1944, the Germans were being defeated on both Eastern and Western fronts, and our hopes were higher than they had been.

My punishment—to do the filthiest work in the camp—came to an abrupt end when one morning Meyer came over to me and told me not to do it anymore. My new job was to clean the washrooms. Meyer told me to wear my white washroom "arbeiter" armband on top of my red *flitzer* band thereby concealing it and causing the SS guards to forget my prior image as an "escapee." I obliged happily and silently thanked God for sending me Meyer, my savior.

The days in the Kazerne Dossin were not as monotonous as in hiding. The Germans, we learned, were pushed back in Russia and Italy and the army of suicide-victim Field Marshall Erwin "Desert Fox" Rommel (1891–1944), was in shambles.* Delighted to hear of German failures, we were nevertheless disappointed and confused why these defeats did not stop the Nazi war against the Jews. Nazi Germany's

---

* Editors: Erwin Rommel was a popular German Army field marshal who led the German opposition to the Allied invasion of Normandy. Rommel was implicated in a 1944 plot to assassinate Adolf Hitler. Due to Rommel's popularity and status, Hitler offered him the choice to commit suicide instead of having his reputation defamed (and his staff and family killed) after a public trial for treason. Rommel committed suicide in October 1944.

goal to annihilate all of Europe's Jews did not appear, to us, to weaken with their military losses.

The searches for Jews and their arrests continued unabated. Jews continued to be trucked into the Kazerne Dossin and preparations had begun for the 25th transport to Auschwitz which was scheduled to depart on May 19, 1944. Because the Nazis could not muster so many Jews, the 25th transport would have to be smaller. Around 500 victims would be sent to Auschwitz rather than the customary 1,000.

Worrisome as this [was], my family kept busy monitoring news from the fronts—this was our main preoccupation. Sometimes news came from Tuchmayer and "his" Wehrmacht soldiers, or from reading between the lines in the *Brüsseler Zeitung* or other French-language traitorous Nazi newspapers that somehow landed in our hands.

In the middle of everything, a strange, near-solution to my looming deportation problems suddenly emerged one morning as we all lined up for the daily roll call (*appel*). Frank addressed us prisoners and announced that the center of Mechelen as well as the train railways were bombed. British ordnance, he said, remained unexploded and was deeply embedded in the ground. He required 25 volunteers to dig out the unexploded bombs and he said that as a reward for performing this dangerous task, the volunteers would not be deported and would instead be sent to an "easy" camp in Limburg (a Belgian province) for the remainder of the war.

Volunteers who believed this quickly raised their hands, and then, looking at me and Silbershatz with our "guilty" red armbands (mine must have shown enough to remind Frank), Frank said that "these two *flitzers*" have to be among the twenty-five. So, in the next few early mornings guards of the Wehrmacht came to the camp to pick us up and escort us to the bombed-out area in the town of Mechelen. It was very pleasant to be out of the camp and to walk around the city of Mechelen. The weather was nice.

Once at the site, an officer of the *Luftwaffe*, wearing the typical German military coat and hat, and with a curt business-like expression, was waiting for us. Speaking in German, the officer explained that we had to dig out the ordnance, unexploded bombs buried in the ground which weighed between 250 and 500 kilos. The officer explained how to do the work by placing heavy chains around the dug-out bombs.

Then Luftwaffe soldiers, he said, would disarm the unexploded ordnance by removing the triggers and finally, pull them out with a crane. Emphasizing the "danger" of the mission, the Germans gave us picks and shovels and warned not to hit the trigger on the very top of the bombs because these devices might explode, killing us all.

Our guards and escorts were elderly Wehrmacht soldiers. Normally chatting with these men was forbidden but my guard, a middle-aged man, started up a conversation in German with me by asking about my family, profession and other mundane matters. The man, a coal merchant from Hamburg who said that he had many Jewish customers, was my guard every day for the three weeks [during] which we worked on the bombs, and we became friendly. At some point, he even brought me work clothes because I was working in a navy striped, custom-made suit—the clothes I had in the camp—and he said it was too good to ruin such fine clothing by digging out bombs.

I confided in him that I was afraid of being deported to Poland and of being gassed with all the other Jews. At the mere mention of the word "gas," he got upset and said that my concerns were the result of foreign propaganda spread by "our enemies." "Do you believe we are animals who go around killing innocent people? We are civilized people, and we would not do that. An intelligent, young man like you should not believe it." I believe he was sincere and did not know the truth.*

The scene repeated itself daily. Many times, there were air raids while we were working during which the guards would run away, and we ran into a shelter. These moments provided us with an opportunity to escape (for those who had guts) and, indeed, five men ran off. I

---

* I.C.: Of course, I wonder now: Did he think it was "right" to imprison me and force me to do slave labor like digging out bombs?

could not escape because my family was in the Kazerne Dossin camp, and I was worried about retaliatory action against them. We dug out a number of bombs and the mild weather facilitated our work. But the escapes cut our mission short because Frank was furious. Of course, all the promises that Frank had made were lies and the men who escaped were wise to disbelieve them.

THIRTEEN

The Palestine Exchange List

WE KNEW THE GERMANS would lose the war but would we Jews survive? In the hope of outlasting the Nazis, my family's main interest turned [to] the exchange list—the exchange of Jews for German civilian internees in Palestine—which Charles had bravely signed us up for. We learned from some prisoners in the camp that their deportation was *zurückgestellt* (held back or postponed) thanks to being on the exchange list and that, in fact, the Germans placed enormous value on it. Though we had once dismissed its value, now we saw this exchange list as our only "card" to play. (In their lawless universe, the Germans were highly unpredictable, and one could never know which rules they might honor but right now, they decided to honor the Palestine Exchange List.)*

Fanny (on the outside) was informed about the Palestinian certificates and contacted a certain "Mr. Rosenfeld" who negotiated the

---

* Editors: See page 165, Netty Gross's "Last Address Unknown: The Palestine Exchange Lists were responsible for saving the lives of more than 500 Jews during the Holocaust" *The Jerusalem Post*, January 6, 1995.

program with the Gestapo to begin with. We learned that the procedure to activate the certificates was as follows: The Palestine Office (in Geneva, Switzerland) would issue a letter declaring that the person concerned was on a list to be exchanged for a German national interned by the British. That letter was sufficient to have the person's deportation postponed to the following transport. In order to skip the subsequent transport, the criteria were more elaborate and required a confirming cable from the International Red Cross, also in Switzerland. To be postponed a third time, a letter had to arrive from Gestapo headquarters in Berlin.

How all this was to be done without phones and while in prison or

Helen (Chaya) (née Kapelusznik) and Jacques Dyner,
undated, courtesy Ken Cappell

in hiding is anyone's guess. But our letter from the Palestine Office in Geneva was to arrive soon after Fanny's intervention with Mr. Rosenfeld, we were assured. It would be valid for skipping the 25th transport to Auschwitz. But would the Palestine Exchange program include *flitzers*, I wondered and worried? My friend and fellow *flitzer*, Sholom [Shlomo] Silbershatz thought so. He was also on the list to be exchanged and was similarly awaiting news. His belief gave me a measure of hope.

In the meantime, the fires of Auschwitz raged on. The arrival of Jewish victims from Brussels and Antwerp tragically caught included my journalist eldest sister, Helen (Hella or Chaya) and her husband, Jacques Dyner. I saw them coming off the Gestapo truck after the customary "visit" at the Gestapo prison cellar on Avenue Louise. They had been caught in their hiding place in a suburb of Brussels where they had been since July 1942.

Arrested with their young daughter, Suzanne, my sister wisely surrendered the child to a Jewish woman (permitted by the Gestapo at certain times) who was employed by AJB. The job of this woman was to circulate in the slanted-floored Gestapo basement prison cell and implore Jewish mothers with children to entrust them to her, promising placement in Jewish foundling homes. Many mothers refused this offer, but my sister agreed to do it, which saved Suzanne's life because young children (she was about 6 or 7 years old at the time) didn't last long in Auschwitz, as we know. Suzanne was sent to a Jewish home in Ashen.*

---

* In her memoir, Suzanne writes, "After my release from prison, I was placed in a Jewish children's home which was situated in a dark and gloomy castle called Aische-En-Refail. We slept on straw and the rats kept us company at night. The children had to fend for themselves. My biggest trauma and fear was that I would not find a pair of shoes in the morning which would fit me, since all shoes were left together downstairs. I remember being locked in the bathroom and having to crawl out from under the door; to this day, I have a phobia of being locked in a bathroom. I never connected with another child or anyone else. I do remember that I was fortunate enough to occasionally receive food packages, which even contained chocolate; these were sent to me by my Aunt Fanny and my aunt-to-be Paula, who married Uncle Charles, my mother's elder brother."

Suzy (Suzanne) Dyner, undated, courtesy Ken Cappell

A prominent Belgian chess master, Jacques would sit in the courtyard and play chess with several chess players simultaneously and
defeat them all. Despite our own pitiful situation, we conceived of a
way to save him from deportation. Like our friend Israel Kornwasser,
who was spared the deportations thanks to his extraordinary skill as
a leather goods worker, making beautiful things which the Germans
coveted, Jack could become the Kommandant's personal chess coach.
We appealed to Kornwasser to ask Frank to spare Jacques who, in
turn, would give him (Frank) private lessons in chess mastery. Kornwasser did approach Frank, and Frank actually came to the courtyard
to watch Jacques defeat ten or more players simultaneously but in the
end declined to help, saying that he did not have "enough time" to do
anything for Jacques.

As May 19, 1944 approached, we became increasingly anxious

about our own futures. Did Fanny accomplish anything with Rosenfeld about our exchange papers? we wondered feverishly. She did.
Certificates were made in the name of "Jacob Kapelusznik and family"
(and Rosenfeld attached Fanny's husband, Josef Finkelstein as a "family
member"); Charles had his own certificate. Incredibly, a few days
before the departure of the 25th transport, we were told by my sister in
a message that our certificate of exchange from the Palestine Office in
Geneva had arrived. That paper would delay our deportation until the
next convoy was ready. Fanny also said that Sholom Silbershatz would
receive a similar confirmation. But I continued to worry: Were *flitzers*
entitled to have their deportations postponed? In the past, *flitzers* had
never been saved from deportation.

A day before the departure of the 25th transport, it was announced
who was being re-scheduled to transport no. 26 and would stay in the
camp. The "announcement procedure" began by Meyer ordering everyone to his or her hall. I stood by the window of the *flitzersaal*, located at the end of the empty courtyard, facing Frank's and other SS's
quarters. At some point, my *steuben elster* (room leader), Mr. Gingold
(a diamond dealer from Antwerp in his sixties, with grey hair and of
medium height) came over to me and asked me why I was looking out
of the window. "Meyer won't be coming," he said, because ever since
the "beginning" [of Gingold's own incarceration] a *flitzer*'s deportation
had never been postponed. "It never happened," Gingold said. "I see
that you are looking out of the window, hoping Meyer will come by, so
I do not want you to be disappointed [when he fails to show up]. I am
telling you in advance that no *flitzer* has ever had his deportation date
postponed."

As Gingold kept talking, I spied Meyer coming out of Frank's
office with a stack of papers in his hand, going in and out of the different halls and announcing the names of those lucky souls who were
not to leave with the 25th transport. I had hoped to be one of them
because Fanny had let us know that we were on the Exchange List.
In fact, Meyer did not come to the *flitzersaal* and I was deeply disappointed and depressed. But not for long. When Meyer was done, and

we could come down again to the yellow-walled courtyard, my brother saw me, smiled and ran in my direction. "Meyer came to our hall (the 13th)," he declared excitedly, "and announced that our entire family—you included—were *zurückgehen* thanks to the Palestine Exchange List papers." Sholom Silbershatz reported a similar story.

Meyer, it turns out, avoided the *flitzersaal*, as he was loath to antagonize the SS who were capable of questioning why *flitzers* were not deported—something that would have been catastrophic for us. But they got their pound of flesh: fifteen *flitzers* were deported and we two remained behind.

As soon as the departure of the 25th transport was announced, a deep pall and panic descended on the camp. By that time, most of the people present in the Kazerne Dossin were caught in hiding places where they presumably had access to radio reports and might have heard the BBC broadcasts which told of the deportation and gassing of Jews. Still, it seemed implausible. True, Jews reasoned, things were bad under the Nazis, but the murder of innocent people, children and the elderly for nothing was impossible to internalize. Besides, the Germans themselves lampooned that very assertion. Indeed, as human nature would have it, the deportees preferred to believe that though it was bad to be deported to Poland, possibly dangerous, gassing "will not happen to us." Later, I read that often five minutes before they died, victims had no idea they were about to be gassed: a "testament" to Nazi lies.

The next day the sinister train was departing and there was desperate activity in the camp. Deportees gathered their pathetic remaining belongings which they brought when they were savagely arrested and managed to retain, and the small bits of food left from their packages. The most pitiful scenes of my life were about to unfold. Old couples hugged and tried to obtain some string to pack their few rags into bundles, and mothers busied themselves collecting food for their children for the "trip." The left-behind prisoners donated their food packages.

Tragically, there was nothing we could do (we had no special influence to begin with) for my older sister, Helen, and her husband,

Jacques, because they had arrived only days before the transport was scheduled to depart. Just hope and pray that the Almighty would protect them. It was too late to do anything for them in the Kazerne Dossin. Helen had a swollen face with blue marks on it suggesting that a violent struggle ensued when she was arrested but when "Horse Head" (Van Kol) approached her in the courtyard on the following day and asked her why she had blue marks she intelligently said, "I fell." It was the right answer and he left her alone.

But generally, SS brutality knew no limits. The old and the sick were thrown out of the infirmary and the dreaded *Shupos*, (aka the Schutzpolizei, or German security police) arrived. Dressed in German military uniforms with strangely shaped helmets, their job was to watch for escapees from a special turret atop the train. The arrival of the Shupos in the courtyard was the ultimate confirmation that the "transport" was ready to go. On the day of the transport, the SS men including Van Kol ("Ferde Kop"), Boden, and "Moshe the Slapper" became total animals.

The deported prisoners had to stand in orderly lines, starting with no. 1 until no. 498. Those "re-scheduled" for the 26th transport were given new numbers. The SS screamed and beat the frightened and intimidated Jews who stood helplessly in the courtyard. Unsure of what to do, the Jews pressed themselves against each other to conform to the orders. Their numbers (large green cards with black lettering) were worn around their necks. This procedure of setting up the transport in orderly lines following numbers, under the hot sun, took several hours. I watched the sorry scene from the windows of the *flitzersaal*. Men, women and children were terrorized and had fear in their wide eyes. (The screams of the SS still ring in my ears.) Boden, in particular, was leading the "horror ceremony" by hollering extra wildly and frightening the already-terrified Jews.

The first to be placed on the train's infamous cattle wagons were the invalids from the lazarett who were on stretchers. Next came the prisoners. After their names and numbers were checked off, these unfortunate people were marched out through the main entrance. The cattle cars were limited to occupancy by 12 horses—or so it said on the cars themselves. Instead, the SS pushed 100 humans into each wagon plus a "refuse" drum for their needs. The trip to Poland, specifically to Auschwitz, would take anywhere from 2-4 days. It's no surprise that we later heard that many babies and elderly arrived dead.

The last car of the train was occupied by the Shupos (Schutzpolizei). The turret was elevated, to resemble a kind of watchtower, so the Shupos could see the entire length of the train and shoot any escapees. The wagon with the *flitzers* was right next to the Shupos' car to ensure that these one-time escapees would not try to run away a second time. Upon arrival in Auschwitz, we later learned, the *flitzers'* wagon was opened last and they were executed at the "death wall." This is the chilling fate I avoided for the time being.

Boden and Frank watched this tragic spectacle with sadistic grins plastered on their deranged and criminal faces. They reentered the camp with happy smiles as if to say, "mission accomplished." What were they so proud of? They were sentencing newly impoverished, starving people, including my sister and brother-in-law, to death. Or, at best, slavery.

When they re-entered the courtyard, Meyer called a general meeting of everyone "left behind" to be counted. Standing at attention as Frank (with Meyer at his side) passed us in review, Frank motioned to me and Silbershatz and asked why "these *flitzers*" were not on the transport. Meyer replied that we had Palestinian certificates. Frank grinned and licked his lips without saying a word. There were very few prisoners "left-behind" and the lines were short for Frank's "review." The mass of Jews disappeared with the 25th transport from the Kazerne Dossin. The 25th transport had 498 victims, men, women and children. The date was May 19, 1944, the day Anne Boleyn, who spent time in the city of Mechelen in her youth, was executed by an ax in 16th-century London, for crimes which historians say she didn't commit. How much would we have to suffer and die for crimes we didn't commit?

FOURTEEN

Schoten

AFTER THE 25TH TRANSPORT left, the courtyard looked empty and sad. The *flitzersaal* was also empty except for me and Silbershatz. As the days passed, new transports of arrested Jews arrived in the camp. The same scenes ensued: the truck passed through the gate; the bell rang for the "old timers" to go inside his or her hall since no one was allowed in the courtyard when that miserable grey truck from the Gestapo rolled in, unloading the frightened men, women and children.

Boden and the SS were standing to receive the prisoners and "Ferde Kop" (Horse Head) screamed *"schnell, schnell"* to the scared prisoners descending from the truck with their pathetic bundles presumably gathered hurriedly during their arrest. None of these victims had known that this would be their last "trip" before their final journey to Auschwitz where most would meet their deaths.

After a few short weeks, the camp started to fill up again. Even though the Germans were being roundly defeated, the trucks with Jewish victims kept arriving—although at a slower pace. As noted before, the Nazis might have been short on trains and manpower, but they did not relent in their zeal to capture and kill Jews, apparently a top priority of the Third Reich. (I later read that the fanatic Hitler Youth and other Nazi troops fought ferociously in Germany days, even hours, before their surrender and Hitler's suicide.)

In late May 1944, Frank decided to send some forty Jews to an "educational" camp called SS-Ausbildungslager located in the Belgian village of Schoten near the Dutch-Belgian border. Early one morning at a line up Frank picked "the forty;" the *flitzers* Silbershatz and I, of course, were the first to go. Also selected were my brother, Charles, and my brother-in-law, Josef.

Before we knew it, a flatbed, open truck rolled into the courtyard and we (the forty of us) sat down on benches. We were guarded by four SS soldiers, each stationed in a corner of the truck. The truck left the courtyard and once again, we saw the outside world filled with streets, stores, people and children. We were reminded of when we, too, were ordinary, carefree people walking familiar streets with no green uniformed, Swastika-bearing beings present; what a good world it was without Nazis! The flatbed open truck was speeding toward Antwerp.

One man in our group was known as the "Bolshevik." I didn't know his real name. He was a giant of a man and very powerful, a bald Hercules. He proposed that we "take out the driver" while he volunteered to choke the four guards. We declined. Though we had no doubt he could have handled the four guards, there was no way for us to get into the driver's cabin which was firmly locked. Besides, it was the beginning of June and the German fronts were crumbling all around. How much longer could the war last? we reasoned. At this point just a few fanatics believed in their crazed Führer, we said to ourselves.

The flatbed truck was rolling through the familiar streets of Antwerp, heading north for the Dutch border where the village of Schoten was located. We arrived in an estate-type place surrounded by high barbed wire and taken to a barracks on the property, constructed of wood with bunks stacked one on top of the other—same as in the Kazerne Dossin in Mechelen. There was no toilet inside or outside the barracks. An SS Sturmsharfuher (equivalent to a sergeant) received us. A fanatic Nazi with a reddish complexion, he was the size of the Bolshevik but also fat. He told us that he will be our leader and that his name was "Schultz."

He commanded us to dig a trench near the barracks and when we finished, he ordered us to get a tree, shave off its branches, and put it across the length of the trench. This, he said, "will be your toilet." As Schultz spoke, he was surrounded by several Flemish SS who would become our guards. The food, he said, you will take from the SS kitchen—a most unpleasant task.

This was an educational camp designed to teach SS how to behave (torturing Jews among their tasks) and we were the sample for them. The most sadistic SS in the camp was a Flemish SS surnamed Van Huffel, with whom we would have many bad experiences. For instance, he later stabbed my brother-in-law, Josef Finkelstein, in his rump for no reason. Fortunately, Josef was taken back to the Kazerne Dossin in Mechelen, went to the infirmary, got well and didn't return to Schoten.

We had to work from morning to evening and in the evening go to the SS kitchen in a basement to peel potatoes and wash the floors. On top of everything, they wanted us to sing while we washed the floors and then screamed "louder, louder" making fun of Jews, keeping us late after an exhausting day of labor in the heat with little food and no shower or running water back in the barracks. The only water available was from pails outside the barracks. Finally, after torturing us with all the peeling and cleaning, we were taken back to the barracks, exhausted.

One day, Schultz asked us to move a 3000-kilo stone located in the horse stable. He asked us to lift it and take it to a different location. However, even with the help of the "Bolshevik," we could not budge the stone. Schultz got angry and said, "Now you are going to lift it with me in addition." He stood on top of the stone and ordered us to lift it with him on top, but the stone could not be moved and Schultz got even angrier and said we would be punished for disobeying him. But Schultz's bark, we soon discovered, was worse than his bite. He was no angel, but when he was drunk, he softened up and called us "my children." At that point we had to sit around him and listen to his war stories.

Life was quite bad in Schoten. The SS were the garbage of the human race and fanatic believers in Hitler. Worst and most vicious of all were the Flemish SS. Traitors in their own country who wore the enemy uniform, they were convinced by Nazi lies that Jews lived from swindling and stealing and forced us to work hard. We worked in the fields, digging the ground and the guards had rifles with bayonets which they kept pointed at us. When it came to the meals, we had to fetch the food from the SS kitchens, where we were taunted and mocked because we were Jewish.

My brother, Charles, a veteran of the notorious camp at Breedonk Fort, warned Silbershatz and me that during the night, there will be a *fus kontrol* meaning a checking of the feet to see if they are clean. How could they be clean, we wondered, after the day's dirty work and the lack of basic hygienic condition? But Charles was not mistaken. In the middle of the night, the guards woke us up and the lights went on. "*Fus kontrol*," they screamed. We had to show our feet to a SS lieutenant who looked at and smelled each foot and sent everybody outside to wash their feet except for Charles, Silbershatz and me. We were very lucky that Charles warned us of this strange torment.

After only a few hours of sleep, we were awakened again and went through what would become a familiar routine. We stood to be counted, went to our makeshift "toilet" (the hole in the ground, with the tree), washed with water from the pail, ate some black bread and went to "work"—digging and cutting branches. The weather was warm, sunny and brilliant. Every day was the same as the day before, only we had no source of news—no Tuchmayer-type to tell us what was going on.

But on June 6, 1944, information on Allied victories came from an unexpected source: Schoten's *Kommandant*. The guards had woken us at dawn and ordered us to stand in line even before dressing. We sensed that something special was happening. Suddenly the youthful

Kommandant appeared on a horse. A fanatical, anti-Semitic, relative of Hitler (according to rumor) he arrived all dressed up and remained on his steed. Then stopping in front of us, he made a short speech: "This morning the enemy's forces landed in Normandy. We will throw them into the ocean together with you Jews." After that, he turned around (on his horse) and galloped away.

The Allied invasion in Normandy (a long-awaited event for us) changed the attitudes and facial expressions of the foreign SS. Hitler's dream to rule the world was collapsing and they worried about their own futures. However, we noticed, the German SS persisted in believing in their Führer.

That day we were taken in small groups to cut branches and trees. I was in a group of five with one SS guard who promptly fell asleep. My fellow prisoner, a middle-aged man who had a kosher fish store, named Mr. Mittelsbach, disappeared. He later told me that he hid (with great difficulty) in a hole in the ground, covered by leaves. He had heard the search dogs looking for him but miraculously he was not found. Next, due to the excitement and disorientation of the SS, four other prisoners escaped, including our Jewish leader, Kessler. He was caught again a few weeks later and deported. Kessler somehow survived Auschwitz, became a landlord in his native Koln, having inherited property from his family, we heard.

The escapes were triggered by the information supplied to one prisoner that the SS planned to close the camp, join the "Deutschland" division in the Normandy front, and execute us before leaving. This information came from a wealthy Dutch Jew, surnamed Prinz, who had a factory in Amsterdam. One of the Dutch SS had previously been his employee and still retained a measure of respect for his ex-boss, (bringing him news and food) and telling him of the forthcoming evil plan.

Upon hearing this from Prinz, panic engulfed us and the escapes followed. The SS fruitlessly searched all night for the escapees using dogs, and were furious at the breach of protocol. The next day, there were several personnel changes as a result—changes which worked to our advantage. Fred, a clever middle-aged man from Vienna, replaced

Kessler. Fred knew how to talk to the SS and even made them laugh occasionally, and our situation improved dramatically.

Suddenly, we had better food and treatment. This was also due to Schultz's replacement with Boehm, a high-ranking SS officer. Boehm, who stayed with us a short time, was the most humane and kindly SS officer I ever met, an exception to the rule. I never encountered another SS officer like him. Once, when we were peeling potatoes I heard him say "Jews are people too."

The next day was the Jewish holiday of Shavuoth (Pentecost). I was assigned to dig a trench but somehow I knew it was Shavuoth. My guard was a Polish SS soldier and spoke Polish fluently. I took a risk and spoke Polish to him. The combination of what was happening in reality (the Allied forces had landed in Normandy) and hearing his native tongue, caused the Polish SS man to chat with me in Polish too, and become friendly. I told him that today was a Jewish holiday (*"Zelone Swiantki"* in Polish or "the green holiday") and being from Poland, he recognized it immediately. "So you would like not to work?" he asked me. "If possible," I answered hesitatingly, disbelieving my stroke of good fortune. (No SS man had quite ever asked me that.) He told me to sit in the trench and promised to signal to me if a German was approaching. I spent the rest of the day not working. From this I learned that there was a pecking order among the SS with the Germans at the top and the foreigners at the bottom.

The German military continued to be pulverized by the Allies, spreading more and more grimness among our jailors: but even in those conditions, one SS officer decided to be sadistic and ordered us to perform physical exercises—an amusement for them and torture for us since we were exhausted from working. This same officer did not like my performance and punished/tortured me by ordering me to crawl around the field on my hands and knees. I could hardly believe that on the brink of defeat, the Nazis would not relent with their abusive treatment of the Jews.

Within days, the expected order came to close the Schoten camp. The SS would be joining the "Deutschland" division in Normandy.

Jewish prisoners were not to be executed but rather to be sent back to the camp in Mechelen. Relieved, the next morning we found familiar faces to escort us back to Mechelen: Von Kol ("Ferde Kop"), "Moshe the Slapper," and three more SS guards. They made us walk a short distance and then we boarded an intercity tramway which was waiting for us—its exclusive passengers. The (now) thirty-five prisoners, with the escorts and guards, boarded the tramway for the ride back to Mechelen. Sholom Silbershatz, my friend, took a deep breath and proclaimed his joy at returning to the Kazerne Dossin in Mechelen which was "easier" than the camp in Schoten. "I am so happy, I could kiss the Horse Head," exclaimed Silbershatz.

FIFTEEN

The 26th Transport

IN THE FIVE WEEKS of our absence, the Gestapo caught more unfortunate Jews for their infernal schemes. The prison population was constantly increasing despite the obvious near-collapse of the Nazi empire. By this late date, the sacred priority of the German war machine seemed to be the enforcement of the Nazi racial laws and arresting and deporting Jews. Winning battles against the Allied forces, (although there were pockets of stiff military resistance) seemed secondary. As long as the Nazis were in power, their war against the Jews would go on, it appeared to us. It was a very treacherous game, managing to stay alive until the Allies—close by, just a few hundred kilometers away in France—came to Belgium.

My parents were happy to see my brother and I in relatively good condition after such a long absence. Nothing had changed at the camp. Tuchmayer was still a one-man news agency and reported defeat after defeat of the Germans on all fronts. The circles around him in the courtyard were expanding. As more Jews came into the camp, they brought detailed reports from the BBC. My morning routine was much the same; running around the courtyard with Jackie the Whistler and cleaning the washrooms.

With all that was going on (Normandy and Dunkirk), the Nazis were making preparations for the 26th transport as if nothing was happening to them in the military field. It was July 1944. They were also readying the camp for winter and received a huge delivery of coal, storing it in one of the cellars. This coal delivery turned out to be a huge headache. Boden and Frank decided that the coal had been put in the wrong cellar on the opposite side of the courtyard. All men (read: [all] Jew[ish men]; me included) had to pass pails full of coal to each other until all the coal was transferred to the other side of the courtyard. When the work was done and the coal was all transferred, Boden was happy and decided to treat participants to ham sandwiches, which he was handing out at a table. (A strange gift for hungry Jews.)

Approaching Boden was very problematic for me. Firstly, Meyer advised me not to do so. Second, I was doing my best to conceal my *flitzer* persona, wearing my red band illegally (according to the Nazis) under my white one (signifying that I was a washroom worker) and avoiding the barber in the hope of letting my hair grow. Now, suddenly, I was afraid that Boden might recognize me from earlier days and wonder why I had not been deported. (If a senior Nazi really wanted to make trouble for you, he could.) A former member of the criminal police, Boden had very shrewd eyes and remembered faces. He knew, for instance, that I was observant of the Jewish dietary laws.

When it was my turn to approach the table where Boden was handing out ham sandwiches, I noticed that he was in a jovial mood. This was not necessarily a good sign. His "good mood" could darken at a moment's notice. Boden was like an animal and [the] Kazerne Dossin was his jungle. Boden asked me what my profession was and I told him, falsely, that I worked in an old age home. After that he said that he was giving me a ham sandwich, *"Aber das ist nicht koscher,"* he added playfully. ("But this is not kosher.") As someone who tried to remain kosher (even during the war), I gave the sandwich to the Dutchman who took care of Frank's pig stall and apparently didn't care about dietary laws.

COMITE INTERNATIONAL DE LA CROIX-ROUG.

GENÈVE (Suisse)

Im Pa Be
FD / lp

DEMANDEUR — ANFRAGESTELLER — ENQUIRER

Nom - *Name* — **JEWISH AGENCY**

Prénom - *Vorname - Christian name*

Rue - *Strasse - Street*

Localité - *Ortschaft - Locality* — **JERUSALEM**

Département - *Provinz - County*

Pays - *Land - Country* — **Palestine**

Message à transmettre — Mitteilung — Message

(25 mots au maximum, nouvelles de caractère strictement personnel et
familial) — (nicht über 25 Worte, nur persönliche Familiennachrichten) —
(not over 25 words, family news of strictly personal character).

Message of 12.4.44 :"please inform KAPELUSZNIK and
family, Office Palestinien, BRUXELLES, they have
been registered on 5th veteran zionist list for
immigration into palestine and exchange. Their
number is m/438/43/52 ; foreign office will commu-
nicate name to protecting power."

Date - *Datum* — 17.4.44.

DESTINATAIRE — EMPFANGER — ADDRESSEE

Nom - *Name* — KAPELUSZNIK and family

Prénom - *Vorname - Christian name* — Jacob

Rue - *Strasse - Street* — Association des Juifs en Belgique

Localité - *Ortschaft - Locality* — 36 Bd. d'Anvers

Province - *Provinz - County* — BRUXELLES

Pays - *Land - Country* — Belgique

RÉPONSE AU VERSO
Prière d'écrire très lisiblement

ANTWORT UMSEITIG
Bitte sehr deutlich schreiben

REPLY OVERLEAF
Please write very clearly

Document from International Committee of the Red Cross confirming
Kapeluznik family on Palestine Exchange List. Courtesy Ken Cappell.

Overjoyed that Boden did not remember me or the circumstances of my arrest, I was also happy that it was already July 1944 and according to Tuchmayer, the Germans were being overthrown. Our morale was high but we were haunted by the question of whether we would live to see the day of our liberation. One morning during that month, there was unusual activity in the camp that would impact some lives quite badly and dramatically. The SS guards, Boden and Frank, were darting back and forth in the courtyard nervously, preparing for something special. Soon the gates spread wide open and in slid a gray Mercedes.

Out of the car emerged Adolph Eichmann's "butcher," SS Lieutenant Anton Burger, who had arrived in Belgium from Greece, specifically to deal with Jewish matters. He decided "that all the registered Jews still in Belgium had to be sent to the concentration camps in the East."

Burger stood in the courtyard with his black boots and legs spread. He had a fat, red face, a butcher's face, and his arms were crossed. In this manner he sized up the Jews. We were ordered to march past him. He reviewed us like cattle going to the slaughterhouse and smirked with a satisfied grin. Later that day we found out that he gave orders to Frank to give transport numbers to all the Jews who had worked in the camp since 1942, including the *steuben elsters, paken tragers,* and most office personnel, as well as certain other prisoners with "connections." All these people were ordered by Burger to be deported to Auschwitz on the next transport and the camp reduced to a minimum.

In the meantime, Tuchmayer was very busy gathering news, mostly from Nazi newspapers. Despite clearly losing the war, the Nazis were preparing for the 26th transport, scheduled to depart on July 31, 1944 and this time it would include Burger's instructions to include all the people who were previously "privileged" such as Gingold, Tolkowski and most of the office personnel.

After days of anxiety, [our] Palestine exchange papers finally arrived from the International Red Cross in Geneva and confirmation came from Berlin. Fanny risked her life going to the AJB, which "represented" the Jews insofar as the Nazis were concerned, to make sure that all the paperwork [was] received and done correctly. Theoretically, the third letter from the Gestapo office in Berlin saying the applicant was approved for the exchange exempted the holder from all anti-Jewish laws until the exchange took place.

Tragically, Sholom Silbershatz, my fellow *flitzer*, who managed to skip the 25th transport, did not receive the letter from the Geneva office of the International Red Cross in time to miss the 26th transport. (There would not be a 27th transport.) Perhaps the employees working at the time in the IRC [International Red Cross] didn't fully realize that a little diligence on their part could have saved the lives of Silbershatz and his young son.

The hunt for Jews to fill up the wagon train for the 26th convoy was on. More victims came to the Kazerne Dossin from Gestapo headquarters—even on the day of deportation! We met relatives and acquaintances with each new truckload of victims, and my father recognized an old friend, Mr. Glickson, coming off one of the last trucks. He knew Glickson, the owner of a sizeable manufacturing business in Brussels, from Poland. It was very sad and frustrating to see people, like the unfortunate Glickson, caught in this net of horrors so late in the war. They would be among the last Jews to be deported from the Kazerne Dossin.

In the meantime, the daily routine continued. In the morning we went to the washroom; then there were the physical exercises; the running around the courtyard; Jack the Whistler; Horse Head and Moshe "Patcher" hitting the prisoners whose athletic performances they didn't quite like. As the day of departure got closer, the unfolding tragedy and the familiar desperate sights took place. People were packing their pathetic bundles and there wasn't much food for the "journey." Of course making it all the more poignant (and horrific) was the news that the German army was crumbling on all fronts, and that there was even a (failed) attempt to assassinate Hitler by his generals.

The departing Jews felt they were in a race against the clock. Especially desperate and dejected was Silbershatz, who didn't receive his IRC certification on time. Having a premonition that he would not survive, he is said to have shouted out his own *yarzheit* from the convoy.*

Frank, Boden, and most of the SS guards felt reassured when they learned that their Führer survived the assassination plot and lived, and they took it as a good sign.† They unworriedly continued to maintain their corrupt lifestyles and carry out their criminal "work" as if nothing was happening to Germany and the Third Reich. In fact, one Sunday, when the weather was mild, Frank brought his girlfriend in his (stolen) convertible Mercedes and took along his valet and driver, the Jew Fingerman, for a spin. Sometimes, when in a particularly good mood, like a tyrant anxious to show his "generosity," he would take off his leather gun holster and put it (with a loaded gun) on Fingerman. This spectacle was performed for our benefit, and while doing it, he would say in German: "You see how much I trust Fingerman? I am giving him my gun and holster and letting him drive me around."‡

In the final months of the war, Frank, a war criminal, cleverly smelled a Nazi defeat looming on the horizon and tried to behave more humanely. This worked to his advantage in his postwar trial. Boden, however, remained a fanatic Nazi and Jew-hater till the end. Boden

---

* Editors: A *yarzheit* is the annual anniversary of a Jewish death, traditionally marked with a reciting of the Mourner's Kaddish and the lighting of a candle.

† Editors: On July 20, 1944, German Army Colonel Claus von Stauffenberg planted a bomb intended to assassinate Adolf Hitler. The bomb killed four people, but Hitler survived with minor injuries. The bombing was a conspiracy of German Army officers and Nazi Party members, who had been plotting to assassinate Hitler since 1942.

‡ I.C.: It is unlikely that Fingerman would have shot Frank. There were SS guards everywhere and any such action would have devastating effects on him and us. Fingerman, ultimately, escaped deportation and survived the Shoah.

believed that somehow Hitler would pull a magic rabbit out of the hat and defeat the Allies. He was the kind of relentless, steel-helmeted German who required evidence of total defeat to acknowledge that the SS was finished.

At this late stage, most Jews in the camp (and arriving to it) knew from the BBC and other clandestine radio stations about the extermination of Jews via poisonous gas at places like Auschwitz. But, again, it seemed so incredible and unthinkable that no one wanted to believe it. The brain just could not accept it. My family was also very worried because my sister, Helen, (the eldest child in our family) and her husband, Jacques, were on the 25th transport and were already in Auschwitz according to our calculations. At least Suzy [Suzanne], their daughter, was not with them.

With the tragic deportations of Silbershatz and Gingold, my hall was emptied of all remaining people. It was very dangerous for me to remain there alone since it would draw attention to me—something I tried to avoid. I had let my hair grow by hiding when Goldberg the barber came to shave the heads of the *flitzers*, and [by] concealing my incriminating red armband beneath my white one. In this manner, I managed to avoid detection as a *flitzer*, whose participation in the Exchange Program's final stages was doubtful.

On the next day, the 31st of July, the date of the 26th transport, Meyer told me not to remain alone in the *flitzersaal* because it could make me an obvious target for deportation. He told me to take off my red armband, take all my things and join my parents and the rest of my family saying, "Don't ask any questions and move now." I did exactly as he said and took off the red armband because I was no longer to be identified as a *flitzer*.

I can't describe my joy at this drastic change in my status. I felt reborn and as though a yoke lifted off my neck. Dagobert Meyer accomplished his mission. He shielded me to the end and thereby played a significant role in saving my life. To reiterate, I had never met him until I encountered him in [the] Kazerne Dossin (nor had he known me). He never asked for a reward and after the war, I never saw him again.*

The lining up in the courtyard was a repetition of the previous deportation tragedy. Each prisoner had to line up according to his or her number which was printed on a card worn around the neck, and fastened with a string. There were six human beings in a row and the numbers started with 1 and went till 554. The SS were wild—maybe drunk—and were beating, screaming and terrorizing the helpless Jews, men, women and children. The line-up took several hours during which the victims had to stand in the hot sun. Like cattle, young and old were finally pushed into the wagons—100 to a boxcar—pushed and beaten with their miserable belongings, and with hardly any food for the "trip."

All who were postponed for the 27th transport (us, for example) were not allowed in the courtyard. But we watched from the windows. I moved into my family's hall and our *steuben elster* was the kindly Mr. Sandzer. Boden and Frank were standing at the main gate and smiling. Mission accomplished—another 554 Jews sent to the ovens of Auschwitz. The last transport from Mechelen's Kazerne Dossin turned out to be as tragic and traumatic as the first. It was a terrible and sad day. We would be liberated just 34 days later, on September 3, at midnight.

---

* I.C.: From the little knowledge that I do have about him, he returned to his native Vienna after the war and had a son there. I once tried to make contact with the son after I learned that Dagobert Meyer himself had died but nothing came of it.

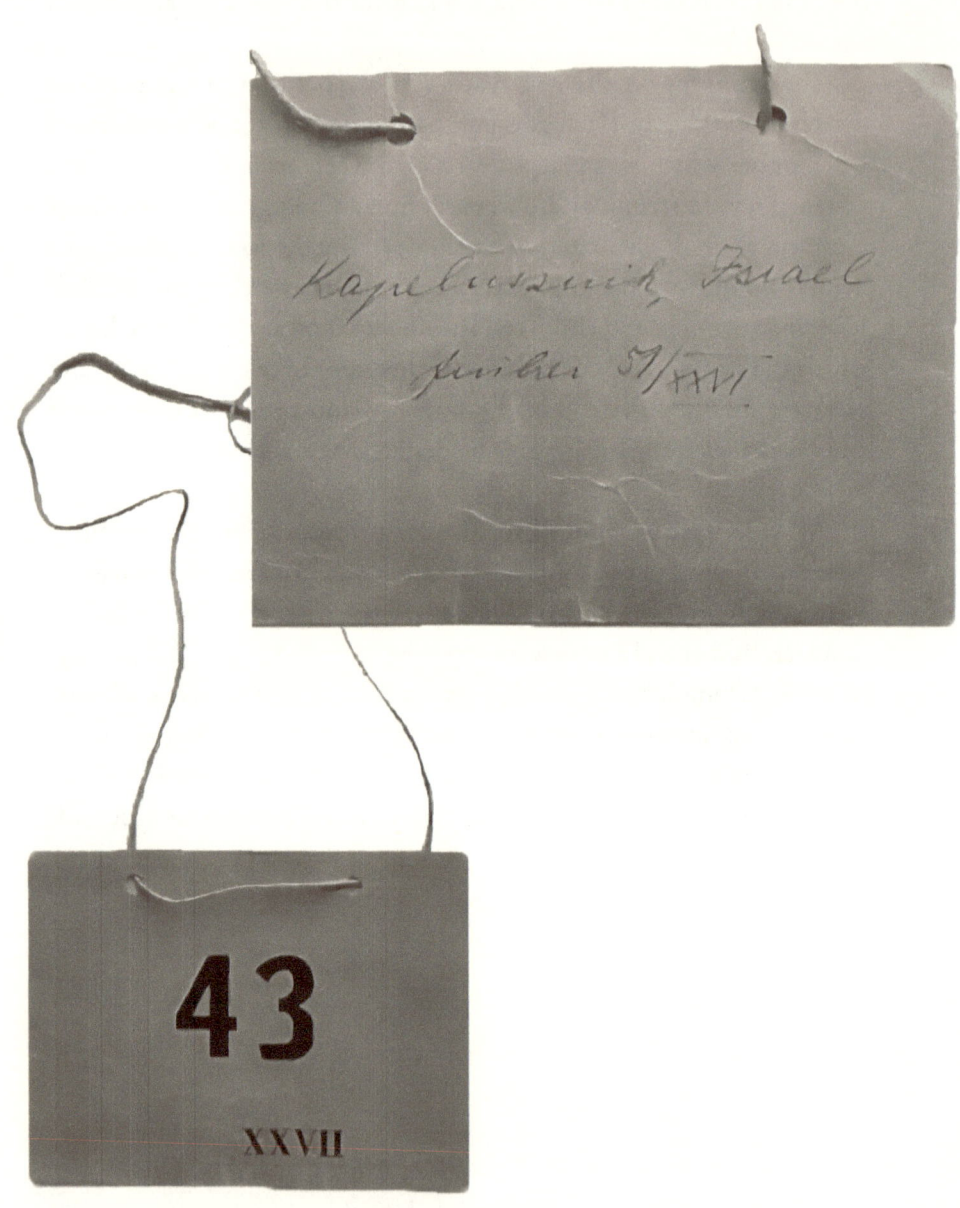

Israel Cappell's numbered placard (back and front), designating
him for the 27th transport from Kazerne Dossin to Auschwitz
after he had been deferred from the 26th transport.

SIXTEEN

Freedom

THE NEXT MORNING WAS ROUTINE. The 26th transport was gone along with Jackie the Whistler, the Dutch Jew who almost made it, and the camp was very, very, quiet. Despite their visible defeat, the Gestapo continued sending trucks with more Jews. I felt partly liberated already because I was out of the *flitzersaal* and no longer designated to be a *flitzer*. But we felt very anxious about the battle in Normandy. Tuchmayer was very busy with his news gathering enterprise. Despite the on-going arrival of more Jewish victims, we suspected that there would not be a sufficient number of prisoners for a transport although the Gestapo was "creative" in the last 30 days in gathering victims.

The recently arrested included some of the AJB board members and its president, Rabbi Ullman, his wife and daughter, and members of the Jewish Community (which was still functioning partially to everybody's amazement). By the end of August, the Gestapo had managed to gather some 500 Jews, enough to form the 27th transport from Mechelen to Auschwitz.

The days were filled with feverish anxiety and every detail of news was devoured at once. Finally, we heard [that] in Normandy, the

Germans' defense lines had broken down and the Allies were moving toward Paris. The tension inside the camp was mounting daily. Is it possible, we asked each other, that we will live to see our liberation, that we will come out alive from this hell? As long as we were in Nazi hands, we did not know what they planned on doing with us when they departed. Were they going to take us with them? Shoot us? Not surprisingly, we were "experienced" with Nazi methodology, and these macabre thoughts passed through our minds.

One morning at the end of August 1944, the gate of the camp opened wide. Was it another future transport of Jews? No, this time it was a caravan (not just one) of cars and trucks moving into the court-yard. The "guests" were the Gestapo of Lille (in northern France) and high-ranking SS police officers. They came as refugees to join Frank and Boden and the rest of the SS guards. Their faces were angry and murderous and filled us with dread and doom. But by now the Allies were flying sorties [bombing raids] during the daytime, and during the night they came low over the roofs but refrained from shooting at us. Maybe they knew it was a camp because they could clearly see the people in the courtyard, nor did they fire on the gray trucks of the Gestapo forces of Lille.

That night the "guests" slept over in the nearby Wehrmacht bar-racks and in the morning Boden and Frank sent them to town to loot whatever they could. They returned with two huge trucks loaded with goods, intending to take them wherever they fle[d].

By the time preparations were done for their departure, it was nightfall and the Nazis decided to sleep over again. It was September 2, 1944, and the Allies were in Paris. We later learned that the Americans and British troops were on their way to Brussels with only sporadic German resistance and no air protection. The next day, September 3, was going to be the last time we would see Nazis, but we were still full of anxieties regarding our fates.

As the Nazis were making their final departure preparations, the motor of one of the trucks filled with looted merchandise started to burn. The SS driver called out frantically for a mechanic among the Jews. Out stepped a Viennese Jew named Rosenberg who presented himself as a mechanic. He promptly extinguished the fire and started to work on the disabled truck, trying to repair it. But after a while, he declared the motor to be beyond repair and the SS decided to abandon the truck, inviting the Jews to take what they wanted. Afraid to argue with them, we all trooped down to the courtyard, and I received a case of shaving soap and a box of blades.

On my way to the hall, I was stopped by "Moshe the Slapper." This time he did not slap but rather cried to me. He complained that he had to leave his family and go with the Germans to Holland, and he did not know what will happen to him. Hot tears rolled down his murderous cheeks. What a pity! Because he was still armed and I was concerned that he could shoot me, I was somewhat consoling and told him, "Don't worry everything will work out."

On September 3rd, 1944, in the afternoon, the bell rang and we were all ordered into the courtyard. Our anxiety was at peak levels, and we were afraid the SS might execute us before leaving. Frank, the commandant, was going to address us, we were told. The complete silence was interrupted only from time to time by British "Spitfires" flying overhead.

Frank said, "We are going to leave you soon. I could make it very simple by putting a machine gun on this table, and killing you all within minutes, but I will not do it. Because when the enemy comes, they will make propaganda out of it, so we will leave you in the camp. This evening when we depart, you should lock the gate because I will not be held responsible for what happens to you when we stop protecting you." Some protection!

Our hearts were beating differently after we heard this speech. This moment was surely one of the most extraordinary in my life. Is it possible, I asked myself, that I will live a normal life, sleep in a bed with a lice-free mattress, get dressed, eat off a plate on a table, while sitting on a chair; walk the streets without seeing an SS trooper; marry; create a family? It seemed too overwhelming to absorb all of this in one gulp but hopes once thought to be fantasies now seemed like realities. For these past four years the Nazi swords were on our necks but no more!

The SS were very busy in the courtyard with last-minute preparations for their departure and did not bother any longer with the Jews, long their obsession in tormenting and killing. They had, it seemed, their own problems to deal with. Boden and Frank dressed in battle gear with grey helmets and automatic rifles strapped over their shoulders. We were very careful not to show any enthusiasm for their defeat which could, in turn, provoke them to execute us out of rage and disappointment. We stayed in our halls and did not show our faces in the courtyard except for the few Jews designated to help them in packing their looted objects.

After darkness fell and the hour approached midnight, the main gate of the camp was opened wide. These were the final seconds of Nazi occupation, and we were amazed to be alive to witness this miraculous moment. The Gestapo formed a convoy and departed. The camp was now *"Nazi-rein"* (N.G.: a play on words *"Juden-rein* or *"*free of Jews," says the author.) The Nazi departure was truly an incredible time, and it would be hard for anyone who hasn't lost their freedom to imagine it. We felt as if we were given a second chance at life. It was a holiday for us.

We were eager to get out of the hellish barracks, from which so many of our friends and relatives had gone to Auschwitz and vanished. Suddenly, a car entered the main gate and to our great surprise (because it was so early in the morning) a delegation of Jews from Brussels emerged. They had come to distribute money to each prisoner. The head of the delegation was Fela Perelman, wife of a Professor Chaim Perelman at the University of Brussels and a childhood friend of my deported sister, Helen, whose fate was unknown to us at this stage.

Originally from Lodz, Fela's father was friendly with mine. She and her delegation gave each ex-prisoner 5,000 Belgian francs and double to my father for old time's sake. The group advised us that a large crowd of Belgian looters had gathered outside the gate and were waiting to enter the camp and grab whatever the SS didn't take with them. Indeed, if we expected a crowd with bouquets of flowers or someone from the church to welcome us—the remnant of the Jewish population—we would be sorely disappointed. Besides Fela and her delegation, there was nobody from the Belgian government, royal family, Red Cross, Catholic or Protestant churches or social organizations there to welcome us back into society.*

The exodus to get out of the camp started at 9:00a.m. Several brawny Jewish men were selected to stand in front of the entrance to the camp with sticks to protect us from the looters. We started to move out past the huge old wooden door which was, this time, wide open. Suddenly, unbelievably, we were breathing the air of freedom and it made me think of the writings of the great Polish nationalist writer and "freedom" poet, Adam Mickiewicz (1798–1855) who said: "Only the person who has lost freedom can appreciate" its return. In our case, not only did we lose our freedom, but we also almost lost our lives! Had the war lasted longer, neither we, nor the Jews assembled for the 27th transport, would have survived. Instead, we would have become part of the Six Million, mere Nazi statistics.

The narrow streets surrounding the camp were deserted, but as we moved towards the center of town, there was more activity. I saw flat-bed trucks with German POWs captured by civilians armed with rifles. The Belgian guards proudly wore armbands with the Belgian national colors: red, black and yellow. One of these armed guards was a man from our camp, nicknamed "Napoleon." He had one leg and helped out at Boden's pig stall. A Flemish-born Jew, more Flemish than Jewish—not that it would have helped him in Auschwitz—he

---

* According to the Kazerne Dossin: Memorial, Museum and Documentation Centre, Fela Perelman (née Liwer) held a PhD in History and married Chaïm Perelman in 1935. Fela established four Jewish nurseries in Brussels after her daughter, Noémie, was barred from nursery school in January 1942. Fela was supported by the mayor of Uccle, Jean Herinckx, who organized school transport to these nurseries and dubbed them "Madame Perelman's trolley car."

proudly showed us the German soldiers he captured and was holding one of their rifles.

The more we advanced into the main streets, the more people we saw. Finally, by 10:00 a.m. we heard a loud roar of approval. British tanks were rumbling toward Mechelen to liberate the once-important medieval city, and its present-day citizens were overjoyed. A large group of Kazerne Dossin Jews waved and stopped the first tank and one of the English-speakers among us managed to shout to the soldier atop the tank that they had liberated us from a Nazi concentration camp. The British soldier did not seem very impressed and told us that he was calling his commander to relay what we had said while at the same time, some in our group kissed the metal tank. All the diversions threw the soldier off for a moment and then he said something to the effect of, "Now please step out of my way because I have to pursue the enemy."

That was our joyous (I am not being sarcastic here—we were very joyous) encounter with our liberators but the soldier's seemingly in-different reaction underscores how little was known about the lethal Kazerne Dossin or about our desperate fight to out-last the Nazis. Remembrances of the moments in which I gained back my freedom remain etched in my memory forever and are unforgettable to me. September 4, 1944 is my second birthday. Only with many miracles did I escape the fate endured by my friend and fellow *flitzer* Sholom Silber-shatz, whom I had earnestly hoped would survive too. After all, he was so close to the finish line; he had almost made it.*

---

* Ken Cappell: We later learned that upon arrival at the death camp, the Nazis pulled Silbershatz from the train, saw he was a *flitzer*, and prepared to shoot him. As they dragged him towards the execution wall, Silbershatz yelled, "Remember my *yarzheit*!" Using records as to when the 26th transport arrived at Auschwitz, we determined this date to be the 13th of Av in the Hebrew calendar. I say the Kaddish memorial prayer for him every year on this date.

SEVENTEEN

Life Resumes

WE TRIED NOT TO dwell on the many tragedies, cruelties, degradations and tortures that we had witnessed over the months of imprisonment, and joyously walked around in the center of town, thrilled to be free and breathe the fresh air without fear of the sight of Nazis marching in the streets, or the frightful Gestapo in their long cars. This time it was the Germans who were on the run, full of fears and worries, and we could not be happier.

We started to look for ways to get back to Brussels which was about 25 kilometers away from Mechelen, but we were informed that the main bridges had been blown up and that there was no transportation to Brussels. We would have to sleep over in Mechelen. By some stroke of luck, a Flemish man approached us and offered to take in our family—my parents, brother, brother-in-law, and me—to his house, offering us food and lodging. He brought us home to the immense surprise of his wife, who also welcomed us warmly and saw to all our needs. We were happy to have found good, welcoming and kind-hearted hosts. They were people of modest means but did all they could, and we were comfortable and grateful.

During the night, we saw fires to the north in the vicinity of Antwerp, from our windows. The Germans were putting up stiff resistance, it seemed. We had to stay with our Mechelen hosts for two nights until the streets were habitable. We finally left our hosts and began walking in the streets when we suddenly noticed a truck with rows of wooden benches. The truck bore a sign which said "Brussels." The driver demanded 500 Belgian francs per passenger, a princely sum which made the ride quite expensive, but we had some money from Fela Perelman, and we boarded the bus.

After a short ride, we arrived in Brussels and the driver dropped us off on Rue Van der Stichelen in the Molenbeek section of Brussels. In a small apartment on this street, my second oldest sister, Regine Dyner lived and hid during the war. Fanny Finkelstein, my other sister, found refuge here too. To greet us, both Regine and Fanny rushed downstairs. The encounter was very moving, not unlike a celebratory homecoming from the military, prison or war. It was as if we had all come back from the Other World—the one from which no one comes back.

Tears and kisses mingled with feelings of relief and disbelief. We were all alive after four years of hell during which Helen and Jacques were torn from us; Charles lost his beloved first wife and my parents (they were yet to find this out for sure) lost many siblings, nieces, nephews, uncles, aunts, cousins, and children of cousins. Good friends (and their families) perished in Poland and vanished from the streets of Brussels. Clearly, our world had been taken from us and destroyed. The full extent of this destruction, and the enormity of the Shoah, was yet to become clear.

But we were very much alive. It was a miracle. We beat the odds set by the Nazi beast. Now, we had to find Helen, Jacques, and Suzy, and a place to live. The war was not over everywhere and would rage on for several more months with Hitler claiming that he would win and the fanatic Nazis believing him. In retrospect, the belief in Hitler was so unshakeable that until they experienced a total defeat and capitulation of the Third Reich, the Nazis kept on fighting and killing—that's my recollection. In my view, Germany had this relentlessness in common with Japan.

After the hugging and kissing, we went up to Regine's cramped living quarters which were to become our apartment too until we found our own place. Our old furniture was put in storage in a warehouse and had to be claimed. It soon became apparent to us that we could not stay with Regine beyond a short while for lack of space. We slept on the floor, scratched together some food from the money which we received from Mrs. Perelman and spent most of our time frustratingly searching for an apartment.

It was a tough assignment to find a rental because few apartments were available. No new construction had taken place during the war years, and the so-called "Jewish" apartments were now occupied by Belgians. Jews who sought to regain their rightful property faced court lawsuits and lengthy procedures. Our impression was that many Belgian landlords had become "infected" with Nazi propaganda and refused to rent to Jews. After looking high and low, we finally found a potential apartment for rent in the Scharbeeck section of Brussels, at 89 Avenue Albert Giraud.

The owners of the house where the apartment was located were two sisters and their elderly mother. When they noticed that we, clearly Jewish, were interested they looked at each other as if to say, "what do we do now?" Seeking the advice of their elderly mother, the younger sister, Julia, emerged smiling after a short while; her mother agreed to rent the apartment to Jews. Julia turned out to be a kind and good-hearted person.

Now, we needed to furnish the rooms and the Feguennes Warehouse was our next stop. When we arrived, Feguenne, the owner, seemed very surprised. This horrid, uncivilized reaction to our survival and return, was sadly not uncommon. He greeted us with words like, "I thought all the Jews were killed?" But he made no special problems and returned the furniture after we paid the charges for storage.

Now we had an apartment and furniture and we started to live again like normal people, and we slept on mattresses, not lice-and flea-infested straw bags. We valued every moment of being free and breathing free air. After settling in, we went to Mr. Moreau, the kindly banker who helped us by saving our valuables and selling them off for us. Two years in hiding was paid for with funds that Moreau favorably and honestly obtained for us.

However, when we came to pick up the remainder of our valuables, Moreau was a changed man and behaved in a terrible and heartless manner. He, too, expressed angry surprise that we were alive. "I can't believe that you are here," he said, practically banging his fist on the table. "They said that the Nazis killed all the Jews and here you are." He gave us what was ours, but his hostile attitude stunned us and remained with us. What a disappointment he was after all that we had gone through! But our "surprises" were not over. While we were imprisoned in [the] Kazerne Dossin, fighting for our lives, some of our fellow non-Jewish citizens were (prematurely) dividing up our possessions.

Next, Charles and I went to our old hiding place and found Madame Carlier and her lover, the shoddy, middle-aged, bespectacled Mr. Paquet, still living there in the neighborhood of Ixelles. They, too, were extremely shocked to see us, staring at us in disbelief as if we landed from some other planet. We came to collect pieces of gold and diamond jewelry which we hid and left in the house. They denied seeing, knowing, or possessing any such jewelry. We did not believe them and filed a complaint in a nearby police station. The police chief announced that we could go to the house and would allow us to inspect the premises.

The jewelry that had been hidden was gone but we found our mother's gold and pearl ring from her wedding in 1908 in Poland under the seat of an upholstered chair. The ring had been given to her by her parents and was part of the cache of hidden jewelry. The police chief took it and said he was handing [it] over to a judge who would decide its fate and we hired an attorney.

Mrs. Carlier brought a false witness to court who swore that she saw Mrs. Carlier's father gave her the ring. The attorney said he was "fed up" with the parade of false witnesses appearing in the courts in those days and advised us not to waste our time with our sad case which could, he warned, "drag on for years." Though the loss of the jewelry was a blow to us, both materially and emotionally, we accepted the legal advice, went back to work, and let Mrs. Carlier keep the stolen jewelry.

EPILOGUE

Justice?

AT SOME POINT AFTER our liberation, Charles went to pick up Suzy, as we called her, with a motorcycle which had an extra side-seat. She was in a hospital with an ear infection. Jacques Dyner's name was, sadly, not posted by the Red Cross—a sign that he perished, and survivors later said he died on the "death march." But his wife, Helen, our older sister, miraculously survived by finding a job in Auschwitz as a seamstress and maid to the wife of an SS officer, who made sure she had adequate food.

Helen turned up in Brussels in May 1945, eight months after we came home. Her hair was short and Suzanne balked at the idea of going to her but eventually they reconciled. Helen continued to search but did not find Jacques's name on the Red Cross lists or anywhere and eventually she remarried a kindly German Jew. With Suzy, they immigrated to Patterson, New Jersey. Suzanne grew up in the United States and married a brilliant rocket scientist, had two children and became a French teacher.

The barbaric Phillip Schmitt, the *Kommandant* of Breedonk,

where Jews and non-Jews were tortured and killed, and of [the] Kazerne Dossin (before Frank), was condemned to death by hanging.

Van Kol, the "Ferde Kop" was also executed.*

Hans Frank, a murderer if there ever was one, received a mere 12 years but barely served several months.†

Max Boden, also a murderer, received the same sentence and [he], too, was immediately released.

SS Journée, and the man we called "Moshe Patcher," vanished in Germany and were never punished to the best of my knowledge.

Lenient, doubting Belgian prosecutors were part of the problem in catching Nazis. For example, I was summoned by a prosecutor to testify about Frank and Boden. I told the prosecutor that Boden was a vicious, brutal man, that he had beaten me mercilessly upon my arrival at the camp after a complaint from Berlin arrived about allegedly trying to push an SS off the roof. Aside from that, I told the prosecutor that I had witnessed Boden kick a pregnant woman in the belly area. She had come off a truck from the Gestapo HQ and was headed for Auschwitz. However, the prosecutor minimized my accusations and tried to dissuade me from testifying although there was a trial.‡

In Brussels, in Anderlecht, there is a monument with the names of all the Jews who died in Auschwitz—many Belgian citizens as well as the citizens of other lands including Poland, Germany, Holland,

---

* Editors: According to the Kazerne Dossin: Memorial, Museum and Documentation Centre, Van Kol was sentenced to death in October 1944 but successfully appealed.

† Editors: According to the Kazerne Dossin: Memorial, Museum and Documentation Centre, Johannes Frank was sentenced in 1949 to only six years in prison. He was released in 1950.

‡ Editors: In 1947, Max Boden was extradited to Belgium to be tried before the Brussels War Council for his crimes. In 1950, he was sentenced to fifteen years of forced labor, but he successfully appealed his sentence, which was reduced to eight years of imprisonment.

Greece and Turkey. No one protected or sought to help these innocent men, women, children and babies. They faced the Nazi beast
alone. Why did they have to die? Why did my brilliant brother-in-law,
Jacques, have to die? What was his crime?

The four-year Nazi occupation of Belgium was a tragedy for the
Jews as well as for Belgian non-Jews. The Jews who did survive the
slaughter owe their lives to their inner courage to disobey the Nazis
and hide, as well as to the decent and humane Belgian non-Jews, like
Pierre Carnewal, who helped them. May the murderers and their helpers know no peace in this world and in the Afterlife, and may the sav-
iors be blessed for generations, as I was. You know who you are.

MY FATHER

Ken Cappell

I'VE OFTEN WONDERED how a man like my father survived the war. He was softspoken, reserved, and most certainly not a Type A personality. How did he make it through this nightmare? Was it his religious beliefs that carried him? Was it plain luck? The choices he and his family made? Divine providence? His sense of humor? All the above? My father would say it was a series of miracles.

We never will know for sure, but I would like to believe that behind his gentle demeanor he had a strong will to survive that was constantly burning within him and that someone up above was looking out for him.

To enrich your understanding of my father's story, I thought it would be beneficial to know something about his life beyond the war years. Who was he? What was he like? What were his interests?

My father was born on May 4, 1922, in Lodz, Poland, the youngest of five children. His father, Jacob Cappell, grew up in a Hasidic home but was a businessman like his father. My father's mother, Sarah Cappell (nee Taub) was the daughter of a well-known Hasidic rabbi, Rabbi Israel Taub, better known as the Modzhitzer Rebbe. He was a scholar but became famous in the Hasidic world for his ability to compose and sing Jewish songs, many of which are still popular with all segments of Orthodox Jewry. My grandmother took great pride in her heritage and my father inherited that trait from her. Despite this Hasidic heritage, my grandparents raised their children to be religiously observant but with "modern" sensibilities.

My father was who he was raised to be. He was a businessman and was a man of faith his entire life no matter what obstacles were laid in his path. He prayed and studied Torah regularly and always encouraged me to study daily even if it was just for five minutes. He enjoyed singing his ancestors' tunes at the Sabbath table and enjoyed it even more when I sang along with him.

As you have read, even during the war he tried to adhere to his faith. While in hiding, he memorized the entire book of Isaiah, of which certain portions he could still recite by heart even into his late nineties.

The family moved to Brussels, Belgium in 1930. As a teenager, my father was active in Bnei Akiva, a religious Zionist youth group (which ultimately played a significant role in his survival), and he felt a deep emotional bond to the state of Israel and its people. He did not go to Israel after the war because, we assume, he was not prepared for further sacrifice and struggle after the trauma of WWII. Though he never emigrated to Israel, he visited it with my mother many times during their lifetimes and marveled at its people and development.

My father met my mother, Evelyn (Eva) Isboutsky, after the war. She was born in Antwerp, Belgium in a modern Orthodox home. They married in 1947 and remained so for over 70 years. They loved each other and were very much a product of their upbringing and wartime experiences. My parents collectively had nine siblings and, along with their parents, all miraculously survived the Holocaust. My parents emigrated to the United States with my sister Michele, my father's parents and his brother and his family. My parents and grandparents ultimately settled in the Rego Park-Forest Hills section of Queens, New York. The neighborhood was heavily Jewish and there were many survivors living there. At its peak, the synagogue I attended had approximately 75-100 families worshipping there. All but a handful were survivors. It was a similar situation in my school.

I walked with my father to shul every Shabbat for all three services. We spoke about everything under the sun. As a little boy, he took my hand as we crossed Queens Boulevard and during services, if I was talking too much, he would gently coax me to pay more attention to the service. When services were over, we went every Shabbat to my grandparents, who lived across the street, for kiddush and a bite to eat. My father was a role model in how to respect one's parents. As we walked home, he would share funny stories about the cast of characters in our shul. When the weather was threatening, he used to say, "Don't worry, I'm holding up the rain until we get home." While it sounds ridiculous, it never rained as long as we walked.

My father was not shy about speaking of his experiences in the Holocaust. He had a habit of connecting casual conversations to World War II. He wasn't morbid about it; it just was so much a part of his core that it permeated everything he did.

My father never had the opportunity to have a formal education beyond high school, however he came across as knowledgeable and sophisticated. He educated himself by reading newspapers and books. He was passionate about history, particularly Jewish history. Had the war not impeded his studies, I could easily have seen him becoming a professor of Jewish history. Not surprisingly, my sisters, Michele and Netty, and I all developed deep interests in studying Jewish history.

Despite not having a college education, he was very determined to write his story in English which was not his first language. As a younger man he wrote love letters and poems to my mother when they were dating. When my parents gathered with friends, he would write humorous poems that often turned out be the highlight of the party. Undoubtedly, my sister Netty's writing skills emanated from my father.

My father was stupefied by the diversity of peoples' behavior. A stranger would show him kindness in a difficult time while others would brutalize him simply because he was a Jew. He wondered how some could rise above it all while others sank to great depths. Why such hatred? It was a subject that vexed him all his life. In fact, he began to write a book entitled, *The Bloody Cross*, a history of the Church's anti-semitism towards the Jews, though he didn't get very far.

He was a gentleman and a gentle man with a marvelous sense of humor which was witty, dry, and classically Jewish. I once drove him to a bank and put enough money in the parking meter for thirty minutes. When we left the bank after only five minutes, I told my father, "Oh, I didn't realize we would be out so quickly, we have another twenty-five minutes left." To which he responded, "So we'll sit in the car for a while."

He would say "Owning a billion dollars is impressive but owing a billion dollars is also good." I never knew what response I would get when I asked him in his old age, "How are you?" This response was a classic. "I'm old. I'm an antique. I must be worth a lot of money. How much do you think I'm worth?" "You're priceless, Dad," I would respond. "How about a deposit on my priceless value," he would quip in return.

Finally, when he was in his late nineties, I often wondered whether his memory loss had impaired his sense of humor. But after he turned 97, I had the following exchange with him. "Dad, remember you have a doctor's appointment tomorrow." "Which doctor," he asked. I jokingly responded, "That's right, a 'witch' doctor." He paused and asked, "Yes, but which witch doctor?"

My father was very devoted to his family, including his parents and siblings. I recall when his mother was ill, doctors were more concerned about him then his mother as he constantly ran over to her home or hospital room to take care of her. When his sister Fanny took ill in Belgium, and there was no one left there to help her, he went and helped manage her affairs. He felt it was his obligation to remember and preserve the family legacy, a responsibility I have taken on since his passing.

He worked very hard to provide for us and would do anything to ensure our happiness.

When I was a young boy, I recall one Chanukah we were waiting for him to come home with a Chanukah present for the family. The hour was getting late, and I decided to stand in front of the house and look down the block for a first sighting. Suddenly, I saw his figure in the shadows trudging down the block carrying a heavy box. We did not have a car in those days and my father would have carried this box in the subway from Manhattan where he worked. I was so happy to see him and when we opened the box, we were excited to see a new color television! In those days, televisions were not thin like they are today. That image of him walking down the street knowing that he carried that box up and down stairs in the subway has forever remained stamped in my memory as a symbol of his devotion to us.

Despite the hardships of the war years, my parents both lived to a ripe old age and celebrated the births, birthdays, bar and bat mitzvas, and various weddings of three children, eleven grandchildren and nineteen great-grandchildren and numerous nieces and nephews. Since my father's passing three more great-grandchildren have been born. My parents carried themselves with dignity and class and were beloved by all who knew them. I cherish the memories they gave me and the wonderful values they passed on to me and my sisters. I felt lucky to have them as my parents. They were laid to rest in Israel, the land that saved my father and of which he could only dream of when he sat in that little attic studying Isaiah by the light of the window.

Israel and Evelyn Cappell at Ken's wedding
September 1987, courtesy Ken Cappell

A TRIBUTE TO EVELYN (ISBOUTSKY) CAPPELL

Michele Bankhalter

DURING THE PRE-CELL PHONE era, while walking briskly toward the subway station, headed to Hunter College, I suddenly heard a voice calling my name. It was my mother, unkempt, sans makeup, clad in a nightgown and robe, chasing after me.

In my haste, I had neglected to insert my due term paper into my briefcase.

Inexplicably, this memory stands out and represents my mother's essence, total devotion to our well-being, and always having our back. My mother was utterly selfless, it was in her DNA, passed down from her mother, our grandmother Necha.

Considering her personal needs, before those of others, was an alien concept, especially concerning her family. She inculcated her children with the values she embraced—helpfulness, kindness, empathy, and respect.

"Say hello," she would gently admonish when we were tots. Yet her compassion did not mute her feistiness and competitive spirit.

While my mother retained the traditions and elegance of her European roots, she evolved as an independent thinker, a music lover, and an athlete (her tennis trophy is displayed on my mantle).

One of my fondest childhood recollections is returning home from school, greeted by the comforting sight of my mother waiting at the door, as the aroma of the liverwurst appetizer, and fresh rye bread wafted through the doorway.

While my father (of blessed memory) was content to pursue his bookish interests at home, my mother enjoyed socializing and entertaining. As an ideal compromise, our basement was transformed into a night club, complete with a comedian (my father), cocktail tables, music, and mixed drinks.

Countless family holidays and events celebrated at home were my mother's greatest joy. In contrast to my father, my mother was less tolerant of our childhood shenanigans. "Murderers!" she would jokingly shout up to us when Kenny, Netty (of blessed memory) and I were particularly rambunctious.

The years following our arrival to U.S. shores in 1950, were financially challenging, yet my mother insisted on sending cartons of food and various necessities to her brother, David, who settled in Israel under difficult conditions and contributed to supporting another brother, Yosef, for many years.

My mother's compassionate and courageous nature dominated her actions as she navigated through the minefields of the German occupation. However, her war-time experience diverged from that of my father as she and her sister Rachel were Belgian citizens which afforded them some protection due to the intercession of the Belgian Queen Elisabeth on behalf of the small number of Jews who retained Belgian citizenship. Nothing more than a public relations ruse, German acquiescence, was short-lived.

My mother often remarked that when the war broke out in Belgium she was a naïve sixteen-year-old and didn't fully comprehend the potential dangers. Her attitude quickly changed during the early phase of the occupation, when she witnessed Flemish Nazis desecrate her synagogue and torch its Torahs in the street. This awful vision remained embedded in her memory.

My mother was subject to dual incarcerations in Mechelen. The first in mid-1942, was triggered when her parents Necha and Shragai Isboutsky, (of blessed memory) received a summons to report to the camp for "resettlement work." My mother and aunt went to the Judenrat and explained there must be some mistake as their parents were elderly and offered to go in their stead, which the Judenrat agreed with.

My mother and her sister Rachel appeared in Mechelen and somewhat naively believed they had "protected" status as citizens. Upon arrival, my mother, bravely approached the commandant, and declared: "We're not supposed to be here. We are Belgian citizens," and the argument made sense to him. However, instead of releasing them, they were forced to remain in the camp for eleven months, working in the reception office, where my mother recalled "the flower of Belgian Jewry passed before our eyes; it was sad work to say the least."

My mother's eleven-month imprisonment was fraught with harrowing events. While at her "job" at the reception area, a Mr. Friedman, who was known to my mother from Antwerp, requested that she conceal a package of diamonds and return them to him when the prisoners were permitted a walk in the courtyard.

"It was very risky," my mother recalled. "And I could have been sent away, but I did it anyway." Was she motivated by her instinct to help, or as an act of resistance? I believe both apply because she also stuck her hand in fire to retrieve a Jewish book when the SS guard turned his back demonstrating her willingness to defy their orders.

One day her eighty-four-year-old grandfather, Kalman Dimenstein, appeared in the reception area. "For him, I can do nothing," responded the commandant, to my mother's entreaty to spare her aged and disabled grandfather from deportation. Upon discovering that Kalman's son—her uncle Noach—was among a group of forced laborers who had arrived from France in a segregated railcar, and was scheduled to be deported on the same transport (number XVII, October 31, 1942) as his father, she managed to arrange that they be reunited in the same car. My mother surmised that her grandfather most likely did not survive the trip, yet she took a small measure of comfort that at least they were together on that tragic journey.

About midway through her eleven-month incarceration period, my mother was horrified to see her parents and her ten-year-old sister Naomi appear in Mechelen. She bravely approached the commandant on their behalf and miraculously he gave them jobs in workshops at the camp. This was remarkable because unlike my mother and Rachel, their parents and Naomi were not Belgian citizens.

"Hundemutter"—dog mother—was the crude moniker SS Sargent Max Boden assigned to my mother during her first incarceration. "I was given the job of watching Boden's dog," she explained in her interview for the Shoah Foundation.[*] "It was a large German Shepherd, and I was terrified of it. To this day, I have a fear of dogs."

After eleven months of incarceration, due to the intervention of the Queen, all Jewish Belgian citizens (including my mother and Rachel) were released from Mechelen. Incredulously, her parents and Naomi were also released.

The family settled in an apartment in Brussels, where my mother found a job with the member of a family who was employed by the Judenrat and therefore immune from deportation. My mother was present when a Gestapo officer unexpectedly appeared at her employer's home to check their papers.

She was arrested and ordered to take him to her apartment where he found her parents and her sisters, Rachel and Naomi. All were taken into custody and dispatched to a Gestapo cellar. The Germans realized deportation of the elderly and children undermined the credibility of their lies. To dispel reports leaking out as to the true fate of the deportees, the Germans allowed the creation of old age and children's homes.[†]

Amazingly, due to these circumstances, my mother's parents were

---

[*] USC Shoah Foundation Institute, testimony of Evelyn Cappell (née Eva Isboutsky) VHA Interview Code 1501.

[†] Editors: The Nazis maintained several children's and old age homes for Jews as a ruse to show their ostensible civility.

sent to one of these "show" old age homes, and her sister Naomi to a so-called children's home.

However, my mother and her sister Rachel were sent back to Mechelen. Unlike their first "visit," they were no longer working in the reception area but were treated as every other prisoner. They had to wear a card attached to a string around their necks with the scheduled transport number twenty-three, which was to depart in mid-January 1944. I try to imagine the terror my mother must have felt on that return trip, as they must have known their circumstances were dire.

My mother and Rachel contrived a plan to approach the commandant in the courtyard, which was extremely perilous, as it was forbidden. Too terrified to participate or even watch the encounter between her sister and the commandant, my mother anxiously awaited Rachel's return. To my mother's disbelief, Rachel returned with a smile, which my mother described as an unforgettable, pivotal moment. Upon release, my mother was sent to a children's home where she cared for and nurtured a little girl, who called her "Mama Eva." They maintained a relationship throughout my mother's life.

I still struggle to fathom the traumas and tribulations my mother experienced during those dreadful years, which left deep emotional scars. How did she come out on the other side? Through her attributes of compassion, faith, sensitivity, or just plain guts?

All of the above.

My parents' nuclear families all survived intact, indeed, a rare occurrence. Together they erected a Bayit Ne'eman B'Yisrael, a faithful home among the Jewish people, and created generations of beloved offspring of whom they were extremely proud.

Stricken with Parkinson's disease in her later years, my mother was painfully aware of our sister Netty's deteriorating condition amid her lengthy battle with Multiple system atrophy, a degenerative neurological disorder. It was a bitter chapter for our family.

The legacy of our dear sister Netty (of blessed memory) mirrors that of our mother. Netty's kindness and generosity, extended to the deserving as well as the undeserving, was limitless and legendary. Being in Netty's company was beyond a mere social interaction. It was an experience. She possessed extraordinary charm, beauty, wit, and grace.

We were confidantes and best friends. Accompanied by a glass of Chardonnay, our "catch-up" sessions were highlighted by hours of pleasantness and laughter.

Netty's rejection of group think was expressed in her bombshell articles. As a journalist, she covered topics that would shed light on issues that had been swept into dark corners, as well as those that she found personally meaningful.

I continue be in awe of Netty, and my parents, and will be, always.

Last Address Unknown

*The Palestine Exchange Lists were responsible for saving
the lives of more than 500 Jews during the Holocaust*

THE JERUSALEM POST, JANUARY 6, 1995.
Netty Gross

Fifty years ago, my father, Israel Cappell, was interned in Mechelen, a Nazi camp in Belgium, awaiting deportation to Auschwitz. It was spring 1944, and my father, then 22 years old, had been apprehended by the Gestapo three weeks earlier on April 27, in a violent midnight raid on an apartment in Brussels where he had been hiding with his parents, brother, sister, and brother-in-law for two years. Only his sister, who had fled to the roof and hidden behind a chimney, escaped arrest.

In Mechelen, my father was charged with the attempted murder of the arresting Gestapo officer—a capital crime. He was severely beaten and thrown into an underground cell.

The Jewish *Lagerführer* (camp leader) at Mechelen, a Viennese inmate named Meyer, managed to have the charge reduced to that of a *flitzer* (an escapee). My father's head was shaved, he was required to don a red armband and live in special barracks called the *flitzersaal*.

Two years earlier my father's elder brother, Charles, who along with my father had been active in the Mizrahi Movement and was a delegate to the prewar Zionist administrative body known as the Palestine Office, had managed to attend a clandestine meeting of the group. The Palestine Office had bases in every European city where there was a sizeable Jewish population.

"We urged him," recalls my father, "not to go because of the dangers of being followed or trapped by the Gestapo. We did not believe that it would serve any purpose or have any value. My brother insisted on going and though he had no idea what it was all about, he thought perhaps it was a way to obtain certificates to go to Palestine."

At the meeting a man named Nykerk, a courier for underground Zionist organizations, appeared. He explained that the International Red Cross in Geneva was forming a list of Zionist veterans to be exchanged for Germans interned in Palestine. The Palestine Office in Switzerland was organizing the exchanges.

"They hastily put together a list," recalls my father, "and Nykerk took it to Switzerland. My brother included on the list his name and another entry which consisted of my father's name, with the words, 'and family.' We never attached any importance to this list until we were later interned in the camp."

Charles at gathering of religious Zionist Bachad
(The Brit Halutzim Dati'im, aka the "Union of
Religious Pioneers"), 1945, courtesy Ken Cappell.

The Palestine Exchange Lists scheme, as it is known, was initiated after the outbreak of the war found some 2,000 Germans—descendants of the Templers, a group of Germans who had settled in Palestine in the 19th century—living under British Mandate rule. The British sought to exchange the Germans for British subjects trapped in Nazi-occupied Europe.

From the onset of the war until 1941 intense pressure was put on the Jewish Agency by Jews in Palestine whose relatives had been stranded in Germany and Poland. They demanded that the agency persuade the British authorities to include their relatives in the general repatriation agreement worked out between the Nazi government and the British.

Once it became known—largely through the media—that Palestinian citizens were being considered for exchange with German civilians residing in Palestine, the agency was flooded with requests from the US, Australia, Britain, Nazi-occupied Europe and, of course, Palestine. The American consul-general in Berlin acted as go-between for Britain and Germany insofar as the repatriation of British and German citizens went, including Palestinian Jews. After June 1941, when the American consulate in Berlin was closed, the Swiss government assumed the role of "Protecting Power" and was ostensibly authorized to handle the repatriation of Palestinian Jews as well as other non-Germans trapped in Nazi-occupied Europe to their native countries.

My father's inclusion in the lists of candidates for exchange represents a later and more daring phase in the Jewish Agency's scheme, when intrepid agency officials in Geneva and Jerusalem sidestepped merciless British and Nazi restrictions.

By 1943, as an outgrowth of their policy of putting forth names of dependents of Palestine-based "veteran Zionist leaders" who were trapped in Nazi-occupied Europe as candidates for exchange, agency officials began adding to the lists names of veteran leaders and their dependents who were not Palestinian by any stretch of the imagination. Though these candidates for exchange were already incarcerated in Nazi camps—primarily in Westerbork in Holland and to a lesser extent in Mechelen—being on the lists stalled their deportation to

Auschwitz. Several hundred Jews are estimated to have survived the war in this manner—including my father.

"Once we were in Mechelen, waiting to be transported to Auschwitz," my father recalls, "my sister, who was hiding in Brussels, discovered that the Exchange Lists had, in fact, a value. She contacted a Belgian Jew named Schattan, who had headed the Palestine Office before the war. He managed to add my name and that of my brother-in-law as separate entries."

The Gestapo accepted the amended version which, notes my father, "was a miracle because a *flitzer* was not entitled to be on the lists. Meyer gave me a job in the washroom. As a 'washroom arbiter' I wore a white armband which he told me to put over the red *flitzer* one. He also registered me in a different barracks and put me on a slave labor detail whose task it was to dig up unexploded shells."

"The Exchange Lists procedure actually worked in three steps," my father explains. "First you had to get a letter from the Palestine Office in Geneva that your name appeared on the Exchange Lists. Then you had to get a message from the International Red Cross in Geneva confirming that fact. Finally, there had to be a written confirmation from Gestapo headquarters in Berlin."

"Miraculously, we received the letter from the Palestine Office in Geneva that we were, in fact, on the lists. That was enough to be *zurückgestellt* (rescheduled) for the 26th transport to Auschwitz which was slated to leave in July 1944. Having 'step one' alone, however, was not sufficient to avoid deportation on the 26th transport and people who, in fact, had no confirmation from the International Red Cross in Geneva were deported to Auschwitz in July."

Two days before the 26th transport was to leave, my father and his family received confirmation from the International Red Cross that they were on the Palestine Exchange Lists.

"Nevertheless," he remembers, "on the day the 26th transport left for Auschwitz, Meyer told me to stay out of sight, to stay in the bathrooms. We were again *zurückgestellt* to the 27th transport, although after the 26th transport left the commandant, SS Oberführer Frank, who was in a rage, asked Meyer why I hadn't been deported. And Meyer answered, '*Er ist von der Palestinäer Liste.*' ('He is on the Palestine List')."

At midnight, September 3, 1944, the SS and Gestapo assembled the Jewish inmates in Mechelen, who numbered approximately 500.

"They put a machine gun on the table and informed us we were about to be shot. Suddenly, they left. We gathered and said [the prayer] *Hallel* and prayed and cried. Everybody came and prayed, even Jews that had never prayed before in their lives."

The following day the British arrived and liberated the camp.

His inclusion on the Palestine Exchange Lists indisputably saved my father from being transported to Auschwitz where certain death awaited him. According to the *Encyclopedia of the Holocaust, flitzers* were executed upon arrival at Auschwitz and not a single one is known to have survived.

Despite the loss of nearly all his aunts, uncles and cousins, my father's immediate family survived the war. They immigrated to the US in 1950.

It is difficult for me to think of the scheme that saved my father's life as a failure, but historians view the Palestine Exchange Lists as little more than an extremely modest success.

By the war's end only five exchanges had taken place, and only 550 Jewish lives were saved. Thousands of European Jews who could have been candidates for exchange went to their deaths. The *Encyclopedia of the Holocaust* estimates that "hundreds" of women who had visas to enter Palestine died of starvation in Bergen-Belsen toward the end of the war.

Just how serendipitous my father's survival was became apparent as I delved into the files at the Central Zionist Archives in Jerusalem where the lists are stored, in the hope of finding the actual list which bore his name. (I finally found his name on a list in the archives of the International Red Cross in Geneva where he was scheduled for inclusion on the 5th exchange.)

Eight loosely organized files deal with the exchange scheme. They comprise a tragic collection of documents and memoranda which can be added to the ongoing debate on whether Yishuv leaders did enough to save European Jewry.

In those files I found the original lists of candidates for exchange—called informally the Istanbul Lists—as well as lists drawn up at later stages of the war, particularly lists of Dutch Jews interned in the Nazi camp at Westerbork.

According to the Central Zionist Archive's director, Dr. Yoram Mayorek, the Palestine Lists have never been subject to any scholarly research.

Mayorek is in agreement with most Holocaust scholars that the exchange scheme's major historical contribution was that early exchanges from Poland were witnesses to Nazi attacks and round-ups of Jews in Poland in the summer and fall of 1942.

"Their testimony deeply affected Yishuv leaders," notes Mayorek.

Typed neatly, in English, these lists, which initially seem as banal as a synagogue sisterhood register, possess a shattering immediacy. They are comprised principally of the names of women in their late 20s, 30s, and early 40s; their children's names and ages; and their home addresses in Nazi-occupied Europe, specifically Poland.

Some of this sad sorority of Jewish women had been in Palestine, but had gone back to Poland to visit parents, and then found themselves unable to leave after the Nazi invasion. Others had husbands who were naturalized citizens of Palestine, but they and their children remained trapped in Poland.

According to documentation in the files and the *Encyclopedia of the Holocaust*, few of the estimated 700 women and children who appeared on the Palestine Lists were ever exchanged. For them, the visa numbers and certificates which the British authorities issued with painstaking exactitude came too late.

Occasionally familiar names appear on the lists.

Hendla Solowejezyk [Soloverchik], age 49, appears on an August 8, 1942, list as residing at 42 Listowskiego Street in Brezese (Brest-

Litovsk) with her three children—Gitla, 16, Hirsz Leib, 6, and Shmuel Jakob, 5.

She is listed as the wife of Itzchok-Wolf Solowejezyk. Her husband, a scion of the famous Lithuanian rabbinic family, escaped to Palestine where he later became a leading rabbinic figure—the "Brisker Rav of Jerusalem." Solowejezyk and her children were publicly executed shortly after the Nazi invasion of Brest-Litovsk.

In many cases, the "home addresses" supplied by relatives in Palestine, to which they hoped visa certificates could be directed, reflect a chilling naivete.

A note dated August 8, 1944, from Ernest Kuczynski of Haifa and Albert Rosenthal of Tel Benjamin, intended as a reminder to Jewish Agency officials to remember their relatives ("future olim"), refers to Paula Kallman, 34, born in Sensburg, East Prussia, and her children, Renate, 14, and Stefan, 9.

"Last known address Trautenaustr. 16, Wilmsdorf, Berlin. Now probably at Birkenau near Neuberun-Schlesien. Certificate number TA/I/759/42D, date of issue December 1942," wrote Kuczynski and Rosenthal.

Similarly Hanna Weinsaft, 40, of 34-35 Kaiserstr., Berlin, is also listed as, "now probably in Birkenau near Neuberun-Schlesien."

That salvation eluded most of the candidates for exchange was a fact known to Jewish Agency officials. In a telegram dated May 6, 1944. Richard Lichtheim, the Jewish Agency's representative in Geneva, writes to the agency's London office: "Please note that we and Barlas [the agency's representative in Istanbul] have tried in vain during the last two years to trace persons on Istanbul Lists. Most copies of certificates forwarded by registered letters end 1942 were returned with remarks to the effect that the persons concerned left or are unknown while of remainder no definite news. In many cases deportation took probab place [sic] before documents reached addresses. Number and names of those who were spared and are now in camps is unknown."

The list dated January 23, 1940, which was sent to a Jewish Agency official in London, Joseph Isaac Linton, opens with four pages of names of women and children scattered in Poland. There are addresses in Warsaw, Lodz, Kobryn, Radom, Bendin, Lublin, Tarnow, Cracow among other places.

Rachel Kleinhandler appears on this list as residing at 49 Walowa Street. She is being sought by Abe Kleinhandler of 64 Herzliya Street in Haifa.

Mary Spanier appears on the list with her one-year-old son. Her address is given as being in the city of Zloczow, at "the bookstore on Sobieski Street." Her husband, Aaron, was already in Palestine.*

Correspondence in the files reflects the worsening situation of those marooned in Nazi-occupied Europe. Jochewed Gur Aryeh and her daughter Hadassah, four, appear on a list of women interned in Berlin. But a side bar notes that Hadassah was not taken to Berlin, rather she was "separated from mother: interned in Warsaw." Rivka Kutner of Warsaw is also listed as being "separated from her son Menachem, age 10, who remains interned in Warsaw."

Gur Aryeh's husband, Natan Gur Aryeh of Tel Aviv, who was head of the Committee for the Return of Eretz Yisrael Persons, writes, "According to the letter we've received from our wives their situation worsens. Instead of the signatures they write, *Mar-li* [it's bitter for me], *Ra-li* [it's bad for me] and *Hatzilu* [save me]."

Occasionally the vagaries of these women's personal lives affected their chances of survival. Next to the entry of Natalia Menashirow's

---

* NG: Marie (Miriam) Spanier, now 80, survived the war with her son, though not as a result of the exchange scheme. I found her living in Haifa, a widow for the past eight years. She had no idea she was part of the exchange scheme. In one of the files, there is a stream of persistent, often angry correspondence between Aaron and the Jewish Agency. Aaron demanded that the agency pressure the British ambassador in Moscow to recognize his wife and son's Palestinian citizenship. Still on file are his wife's love letters, written to him from Zloczow, which he submitted.

name are the remarks: "An application for repatriation to Palestine was made by her husband but he did not, when requested, furnish a bond to refund the cost of her repatriation." [Menashirow, 33, from Kielee, later appears on an October 8, 1940, list of women interned in Berlin.]

Similarly Lisabeth Loszynski, "the divorced wife of Mr. Alexander Loszynski. No application for repatriation has been made on her behalf."

But most husbands living in Palestine left nothing to chance. They supplied the Jewish Agency with multiple addresses where they hoped their wives and children could be found. There are five carefully typed addresses, in five separate locales—Siemierz, Wysokie, Zamose, Komarow, and Tomaszow-Lubelski—where Jacob Gelernter of Tel Aviv hoped his wife, Rivka, and child, Jonah, could be located.

Perhaps as compelling as the lists themselves is the "list culture" which developed around the exchange program—the barrage of letters, telegrams, documents and memorandums in which petitioners plead for the lives of their loved ones.

In one file there is a telegram dated August 17, 1944, from Linton in London, which states: "Weizmann anxious about Perlberger family. Please answer my cable."

"We understand from America," notes another cable dated August 1944, one of at least half a dozen regarding Claire Perlberger and her three sons, "that Perlberger family was granted permit in January 1944. This family should have been on approved Holland List but unable to find trace of them."

Perhaps the most heartrending pleas in the files come from those men who entered Palestine by illegal means. This meant their wives and children stood no chance of being placed on the lists. In one undated letter, the writers note, "We had no home; the democratic world collapsed and didn't open their gates to us. And those who couldn't emigrate were slaughtered in different camps. If we hadn't succeeded in escaping, we would also be turned into Jewish soap or chemical fertilizer. If a ship sinks and someone managed to escape, does one judge him? No certificates, no visas through Turkey, no Swedish ships, is the reason for our disaster. Just clemency for the illegal husbands who [hoped their] wives could then get laissez-passes [sic] passports."

Among the more remarkable letters addressed to the agency is one dated November 11, 1942, from "A group of Zionist activists from Poland currently living in Palestine."

"All Jews incarcerated in the occupied Nazi areas," write the authors, "are entitled to come to Eretz Yisrael, and we pray that the Jewish Agency saves them all. We, however, maintain that as Zionist veteran leaders who devoted the best years of their lives to the cause, we are justified and entitled to request from the Jewish Agency first priority, special treatment, singular concern and an effort that surpasses all others to save, first and foremost, our wives and children who are deep in suffering, poverty and hunger."

Confidential and Internal

As the only body which represented those Jews trapped in Nazi-occupied Europe who wanted to be included on the Palestine Exchange Lists, the Jewish Agency is criticized today for not bringing the lists to the wider public's attention. Their motives for this remain puzzling, but the obsequiousness with which agency officials addressed the British in their correspondence suggests they were afraid of breaking the tenuous link that existed, or that the British had asked them to keep the existence of the lists secret.

The picture of Jewish Agency officials that emerges from the files of the Central Zionist Archives in Jerusalem is a complex one. But most agency officials, particularly Dr. Leo Kohn and Bernard Joseph in Jerusalem, Joseph Isaac Linton in London, and Richard Lichtheim in Geneva, were continuously trying to formulate schemes which might save lives: Kohn tried to save "five distinguished Jewish rabbis from Holland in Bergen-Belsen" by

As the war proceeded, it appeared that some of the women and children who appeared on the original Palestine Lists were still alive, a fact which surprised even Jewish Agency officials.

On one list, dated December 12, 1944, there is a note from Dr. Leo Kohn, an official of the Jewish Agency, to G.G. Grimwood at the British chief secretary's office in Jerusalem, which states: "I understand, from the committee of husbands of Palestinian women interned in Germany, that they have learned from recent arrivals from Bergen-Belsen that a number of women and children included in the Palestine Lists are actually at Bergen-Belsen! It is clear that if this is so they should be the first to be included in the fourth exchange."

Some names on this list are familiar already—such as the Kozicki (here spelled Kozeycki) family. Originally, Marjem Kozicki was listed with her seven children, and a relative, Beila Kozicki, and her five

arranging to exchange them for German clerics in Palestine.

In a memo typed in Hebrew marked "Confidential and Internal" dated May 4, 1944, with copies to "D. Ben-Gurion, M. Shertok, A. Kaplan, Y. Greenbaum," the writer notes, "We were asked to keep this matter secret. The next round of exchanges will take place in several weeks and will include 280 souls. [That exchange took place in June 1944 and included 283 persons]. It seems that only a small minority have any claim to Palestinian citizenship of any sort and a very small number are from Palestine Lists altogether. The majority are from lists of old-time Zionists of ours at the top of which is Holland."

"There are a small number of names from Belgium and Germany. It seems there is nobody from Poland. The German government for its part promises to continue searching for these people. The [British] Government is also eager to keep this matter silent." - N.G.

children. However, by the time Lichtheim in Geneva is able to confirm these names on a February 8, 1945, list, the Kozycki [sic] family is greatly condensed. It now consists only of Marjem and her twin daughters, and her relative Beila.

Leontine Sarah Kupfer and her three children Ruth-Sara, Siegfried-Israel, and Manfred-Israel, who had appeared on an earlier list, have also disappeared. [According to the Nuremberg Laws, all Jewish females were required to add the name Sara, and males, Israel, after their first names.]

On November 27, 1942, a Jewish Agency employee, Bernard Joseph, wrote a letter to the British chief secretary in Jerusalem in which he stated that, "In view of the mass murder of Jews which is at present proceeding in enemy countries. . . . every effort should be made by negotiation with the German government to rescue all those whose husbands and fathers are living in this country. It may well be that this may offer the last opportunity of saving these persons."

But the British response to pleas of this nature was painfully petty. A letter from a British official, Robert Scott, dated August 23, 1940, to the Executive of the Jewish Agency, asks to be reimbursed for a telegraph sent by the Commissioner for Migrations and Statistics to London.

"In accordance with Dr. Kohn's request," writes Scott, "the telegraph bore the particulars of Palestinian civilians interned in Germany . . . so they could let their existence be known to their families in Palestine. The cost of the telegram was 9,280 mils and I am to request that you will be good enough to remit the amount by cheque made out to the Sub-Accountant, Secretariat."

On September 24, 1942, the same Scott spent an hour with Kohn. In a two-page memorandum of the interview "he explained," notes Kohn bitterly, "why the exchange program originated not in order to save Jews but rather to get rid of 300 German women in Palestine."

Nor did the Swiss government, the so-called Protecting Power, exhibit heroic measures to save lives.

In a memo dated March 14, 1944, Lichtheim informs Jewish Agency official I. Gruenbaum that "the Swiss government has no access to the [concentration] camps and the inmates are in no way under the protection of the Swiss government. The real meaning of the words 'protecting power' means that certain foreign interests have been entrusted to Switzerland. In our case the role of the Swiss government consisted only of transferring the lists of candidates to the German authorities in accordance with the wishes expressed by the British government."

———————

On a recent visit to Jerusalem, where he gave testimony to Yad Vashem, my father visited the Central Zionist Archives and reflected on events that occurred 50 years ago.

"In Mechelen, I was incarcerated with my good friend Sholom Zilberschatz [Silbershatz] who was also a *flitzer*. When we discovered that I was not to be on the 26th deportation to Auschwitz, and he was, he gave me a look as if to say, 'Live for me, pal.'

"I owe my life to those Jewish Agency officials who, as the killings proceeded, realized that each Jewish name they came across represented a human being who desperately wanted to live and who equally desperately needed a miracle to do so. I honor them. Had there been more individuals like them, maybe Sholom and thousands of other Jews would still be alive today. He died in Auschwitz. I consider his imperative to me—to live—sacred."

Journalist Netty Gross, voice of those "who otherwise wouldn't be heard," dies at 66

TIMES OF ISRAEL, NOVEMBER 16, 2021

Janine Zacharia

Netty (Cappell) Gross-Horowitz, an acclaimed reporter and writer who penned scores of in-depth features about the Jewish world, including groundbreaking investigations for *The Jerusalem Report* into restitution for Holocaust victims, died on November 15 in New York City. She was 66.

With her stylish flair, Gross-Horowitz brought a sophisticated, Upper West Side chic to Jerusalem, where she lived for nearly three decades before moving back to her native New York in the course of a lengthy battle with Multiple system atrophy, a degenerative neurological disorder. She is survived by her siblings Michele Bankhalter and Kenneth (Kenny) Cappell, her children Ayala Horwitz, Tamar Freidenberg, Avi Gross and Daniel (Dani) Gross, and eight grandchildren. Her husband, Elliott Horowitz, died in 2017.

Gross-Horowitz worked most extensively for *The Jerusalem Report*, and wrote for other publications including *The Jerusalem Post* and *Times of Israel* during a career that spanned decades.

Gross-Horowitz was born December 18, 1954, in Queens, New York. She attended Queens College and studied art history. After moving to Jerusalem, her home on Beit Eshel Street in Old Katamon became a welcoming den of beautiful artwork and an eclectic collection of empty coffee tins, where Fleetwood Mac was blasted and late-night Shabbat dinners were held.

Gross-Horowitz used her tremendous reporting and writing skills

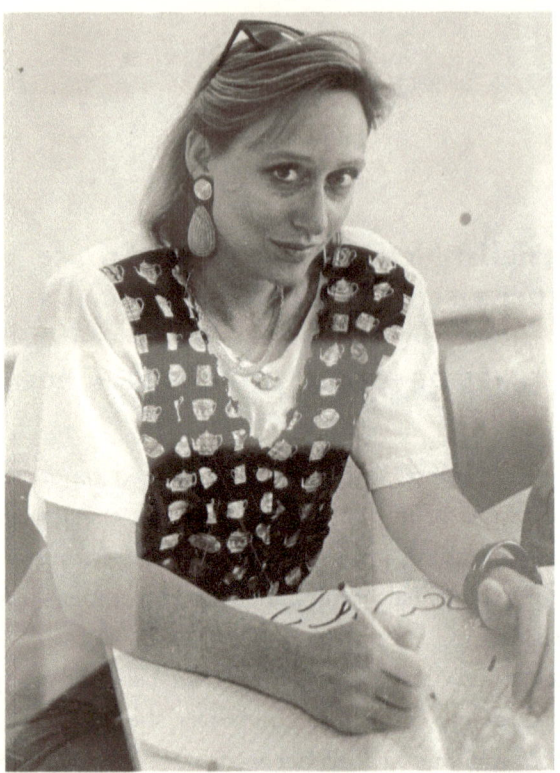

Netty Gross-Horowitz, 1990s, courtesy Avi Gross

to document how her father, Israel Cappell, avoided being deported to Auschwitz in August 1944, a tale involving the Jewish Agency, the Red Cross, and the Gestapo. Both her parents were interned in the Mechelen deportation camp in Belgium and managed to survive the Nazi genocide.

At her funeral service at Riverside Memorial Chapel in Manhattan on November 15, Gross-Horowitz's eldest daughter, Ayala Horwitz, recalled her mother's storytelling skills. "She always told the best—and very vivid—stories. Our family lore is full of stories from her childhood."

Her lengthy and numerous features about organizational Jewry,

Jewish history and culture, and life in Israel, began with cinemat-
ographic anecdotes and pressed on with urgent, compelling prose, as
in a 2008 *Jerusalem Report* feature she wrote about Eastern European
Jews who survived the Holocaust but felt they never "won what they
consider adequate recognition or financial reparations for their suffering and loss of property."

"Rochla Trachtman survived the Holocaust, but she isn't a Holocaust survivor," Gross-Horowitz wrote. "The 88-year-old Yiddish-
speaking woman, blind and wheelchair-bound, lives in a tenement
in Jaffa with a 24-hour caretaker. Sitting in her neat, modest living
room, she tells a visitor that she, her husband Haim and their infant
daughter, Eta, fled from Kishinev, Moldova, on the eve of the German
invasion of Soviet territory, in June 1941. They boarded a cattle wagon,
which took them to Stalingrad (today Volgograd, Russia) on the west
bank of the Volga River. Caught up in one of the bloodiest battles ever,
they endured bombardment and starvation. The baby died in her arms.
But they were among the very few people who survived the Battle of
Stalingrad."

Gross-Horowitz often used her journalistic talents and platform to
give voice to people who "otherwise wouldn't be heard," Horwitz said,
remembering the time her mother advocated for an Israeli woman
named Dorit who was "ignored by the harsh Israeli bureaucracy."
In 2012, Gross co-authored a book that documented the difficulties
women faced in securing divorces in Israel.

One story prompted a reader to mail in a donation. "I don't think
The [Jerusalem] Report ever got a response like that," her long-time
close friend and colleague Sharon Ashley recalled.

"She was not afraid to voice her sometimes unpopular opinion.
And she always stood up for what she believed in," Horwitz said. Her
mother, she recalled, once went to the head of her daughter's school
and insisted that she, as great-great-granddaughter of the founder of
the Modzitz Hasidic dynasty, Rebbe Yisrael Taub, would not be ex-
pelled.

Gross-Horowitz's relentless investigations in the late 1990s into restitution for Holocaust victims were groundbreaking.

"Netty was sparkling funny and deadly serious at the same time," recalled Hirsh Goodman, founder and former editor-in-chief of *The Jerusalem Report*. "She was also courageous. What comes to mind is her seminal work in exposing serious cracks in what we all thought to be the holiest of holies in the Jewish world, the untouchables, restitution to Holocaust survivors. It was challenging as an editor to take the step in publishing, but then who could refuse the twinkle and the wink. 'My sources are impeccable,' she said, and, as always, so they were."

Times of Israel editor David Horovitz, a former colleague at *The Jerusalem Report*, paid tribute to "a warm, kind and considerate friend, who was also always so poised and elegant, and of course an original thinker and so sharp."

"Netty was a stylish writer and a formidable reporter—empathetic, tenacious in seeking out truth, and relentless in challenging individuals and organizations who needed bringing to account. We loved working with her," Horovitz said.

This writer did too. In 1995, I got my start in journalism as a 21-year-old intern at *The Jerusalem Report*. After I was promoted to full-time reporter, in one of the great fortunes of my life, I got the desk next to Netty Gross-Horowitz, who remained one of my most cherished confidantes and closest friends for more than a quarter-century.

At her funeral service, Gross-Horowitz's family recalled her vast talents, extreme generosity, boundless warmth, unparalleled wit, and signature style. Everyone noted just how fun it was to simply hang out with her.

"She always thought about others," said Gross-Horowitz's brother, Kenny Cappell. What she wanted most was that others would "feel good about themselves."

Avi Gross spoke of his mother's "powerful, maternal, unconditional love" and described her as a "glorious, beautiful human being."

Her son Dani recalled that when he had his face buried in his computer growing up, his mother would coax him to go outside, meet people and have a good life. "If there would be a way to remember her by one adjective, I do think it would be energy. She was a very, very energetic person."

After the service, her brother told me how Gross-Horowitz had described her interview with US president Bill Clinton. "I remember, she said, 'He makes you feel like there's nobody else in the room he's focused on except you.' In some ways, I think Netty had that quality too."

Gross-Horowitz was laid to rest at Har Hamenuchot in Jerusalem on November 16.

THE MEMOIR OF FANNY FINKELSTEIN
(NÉE KAPELUSZNIK)

I ARRIVED IN BELGIUM in 1930, when I was thirteen years old. In 1937, I married Joseph Finkelstein. During the first seven years, I spent two years at the middle school on Rue Georges Moreau. Unfortunately, my classes were in Flemish, given that I had been the best student in Poland. At school, I was not interested in Flemish. I learned very little French and there was no possibility to switch [the language of instruction]. At home, there was no food. We were five kids. Given my childhood in Lodz in a rich bourgeois family, I was not accustomed to life's difficulties. We didn't have enough food and I fell gravely ill with tuberculosis, which was incurable at the time. No Jewish organization wanted to help, neither with food nor with money. It was a miracle that I recovered, thanks to Dr. Lemoine who was at that time director of the hospital. Finally, I got better, and three months after, I married a magnificent man, Joseph Finkelstein.

From 1942 on we were in hiding with my parents. It was me, my husband, and my two brothers—Charles, who was three years older than me, and Israel, the youngest, who was six years my junior. We rented a house at 12 Rue de Châtelain. My parents and my two brothers stayed on the second floor, and my husband and I were on the third.

Mme Carlier (Lou) lived on the ground floor with her boyfriend and they took care of the shopping, the food, and our needs. The two of them were considered the sole occupants of the house; as for us, we didn't exist to the outside world.

At 4:00am on the 27th of April, 1944, the Gestapo arrived. There were several of them in military gear, six people in a large vehicle. They knocked at the door with their rifles and shouted loudly. The woman opened the door. They went upstairs to where my parents were and started beating them. They ordered them to get dressed quickly and pack their bags, otherwise they would kill them on the spot. My husband, younger brother and I heard our parents' shouts. My brother hurried to the attic and went out the window and onto the roof, which was very dangerous because it was not flat, but rather and slanted downward on both sides, and slippery due to the icy rain. I went out on the roof, and my only thought was to save my own life and that of my loved ones. I was barefoot and wearing just a nightgown, nothing else, as that's how I sleep. It was cold at 4am and I left my savings in a drawer alongside my jewelry, which included a 4-carat blue-white [sapphire and diamond] ring.

As soon as we had settled ourselves on the roof, one of the Gestapo arrived in the attic. I saw his face through the window. He noticed us right away and said in German, "All three of you come down right away." He took out his gun and said that if we didn't come down, he would kill the three of us. I told my husband and my brother to go down, and I said that I would not go with them, and that I wanted to try and save myself while they were busy going down. I crossed to the other side of the roof, the side facing the street, and since I was young enough and wearing neither clothing nor slippers, it was doable. The edge of the roof was between fifty and seventy centimeters wide, maybe less, so I ran over to the next house, which was the same shape as mine. I climbed up to the chimney, which was the same shape as ours, except a bit more than 50 cm taller. I then lay down with my feet held up by the chimney and I pressed myself against the wall under the roof overhang and didn't breathe. I was blue with cold and fear. Right after I had hidden myself, the Gestapo agent looked out the window, searching for me. He yelled, "She can't get far like that, without clothes or slippers!" and he ordered his men to bring up a searchlight and to light up the area every time he called for me. Without a doubt, the only reason they didn't find me is that I was very thin and pressed against the wall under the overhang, not moving or breathing. Finally, he went out the window and onto the roof, and from my hiding spot, I saw that his boots were sliding on the roof. He slipped and almost fell. He got frightened and went back in through the window that he had come out of, the one on the front of the attic. Afterwards, he went down and savagely beat my 22-year-old brother until he bled from his nose and ears as revenge for not finding me. The sad convoy then departed while being beaten and savagely screamed at by the Gestapo.

Since I was on the roof, I wasn't sure they had all left, so I started to throw little pebbles to see if the Gestapo would react. Because I was so close to the window, when he was by the window—and he stayed there quite some time, watching for a sign that I was out there—I could smell cigarette smoke. When I was sure that the danger had passed, I went back in the window and went downstairs. I found myself facing the woman and her friend. They told me that the Gestapo said that if I returned, they must keep me there because they would be back the following afternoon to look for me around 3:00pm. If I wasn't there, the two of them would take my place. They tried to force me to stay.

During our period of hiding, my brother collaborated with the members of a very active partisan group called "la garde blanche" [the White Guard]. One of their leaders, Pierre Carnewal, was 24 years old like me. He was an exceptional person, who brought us ration cards and food, and was a great do-gooder and friend of my brother's. He was the son of a known brewer from Uele and an English mother, the daughter of an English lord, whose patriotism and generous heart inspired him to save Jews who were in hiding. So, he was known by the woman and her friend, as he would visit us often, which distressed the woman. I understood the danger of my terrible situation, and told them that Pierre would get them back for this, and to not, under any circumstances, let me be taken away by the Gestapo. Otherwise, the partisans would kill them, either now or after the war ends. They were frightened and let me leave.

As I was afraid that someone in the neighborhood might recognize and denounce me, and I had to go out and earn money, I put on my brother's clothing, hid my abundant blonde hair in a men's cap, carried a workman's bag, and put on men's shoes. I took the train like that to my older sister's house. She was in hiding with her husband and a little girl in a similar situation to the one my family and I had with the Belgian couple.

My sister and her husband's despair upon seeing me was immense. I calmed them and told them not to lose hope, and that with God's help, I would do all I could to save them. My love for my family and my parents knew no bounds.

I spent the night at my sister's house and the next morning, I went to look for a place to hide. I found a place right by the Cour de Cessation, also in Molenbeek. I noticed a run-down two-story house with a grocery store on the ground floor. The owner was kind and she understood my situation immediately. She told me that if the Gestapo were to come, she knows nothing of my situation and is not responsible for me. I agreed and got in contact with a member of a partisan group. He got me a Belgian identity card under the name Vanden Kerceef since I was blonde and didn't look particularly Jewish.

The fact that there was a grocery store in the building made things easy for me, as I had the right to send three to five packages every week with the assistance of a Belgian woman, ABG. I did this until Liberation.

In September 1944, I was reunited with my entire family and my husband, freed and in good health, and we all started a new life.

Other details concerning us and my family are long stories with different episodes.

ABOUT THE COVER AND TITLE

THE COVER IS REPRESENTATIVE of the location my father describes while in hiding where he would study the Prophet Isaiah by the light of an attic window. He found Isaiah provided him solace with its hopeful and consoling verses. My father would sometimes muse that perhaps he was saved because of Isaiah. This belief hardened over time, so much so that in his late nineties he told me of a dream where a man with a long wavy beard that went down to the floor was talking to him. He asked a group of people, "Who is this man?" and they responded, "This is the Prophet Isaiah."

My father originally wanted to call his book *Twenty-two Miracles*, but we were unsure how he determined what was or was not a miracle. We then considered many verses from the Book of Isaiah that capture the hope and salvation that my father was yearning for. However, in the final analysis we wanted the title to be as close to his wishes and words as possible and accordingly selected a phrase from his memoir, *With Many Miracles*.

Ken Cappell